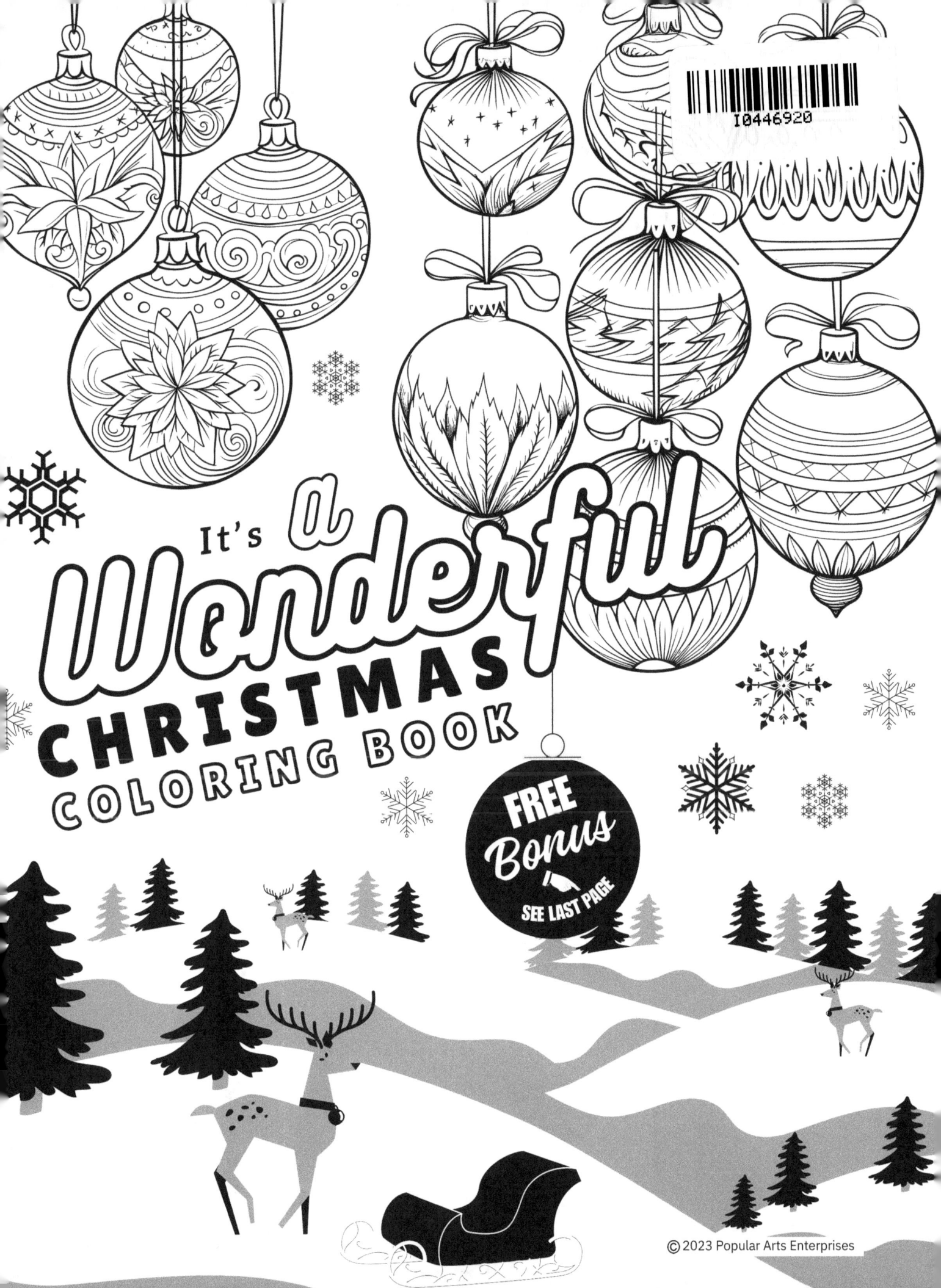

It's a **Wonderful** CHRISTMAS COLORING BOOK

FREE Bonus
SEE LAST PAGE

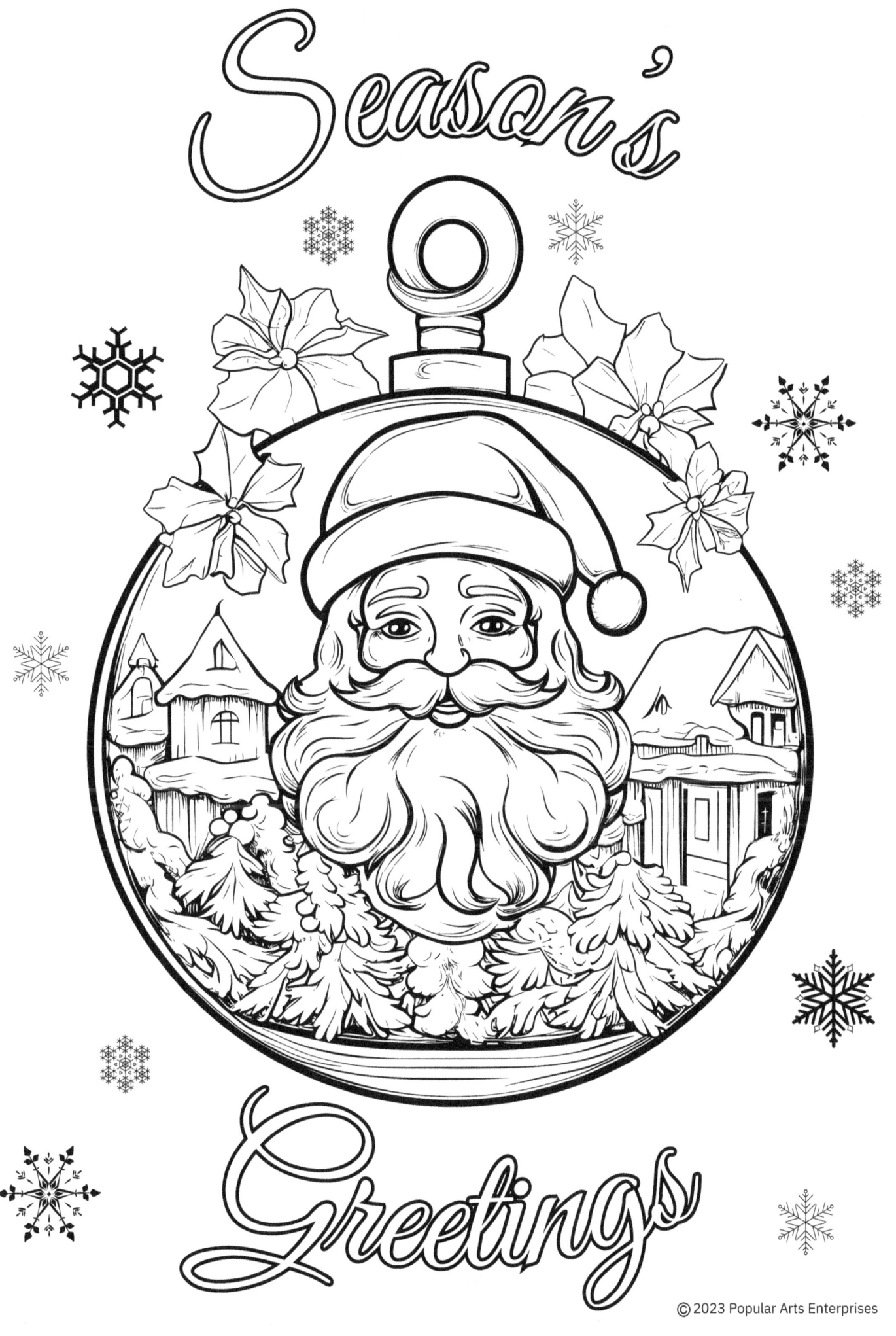

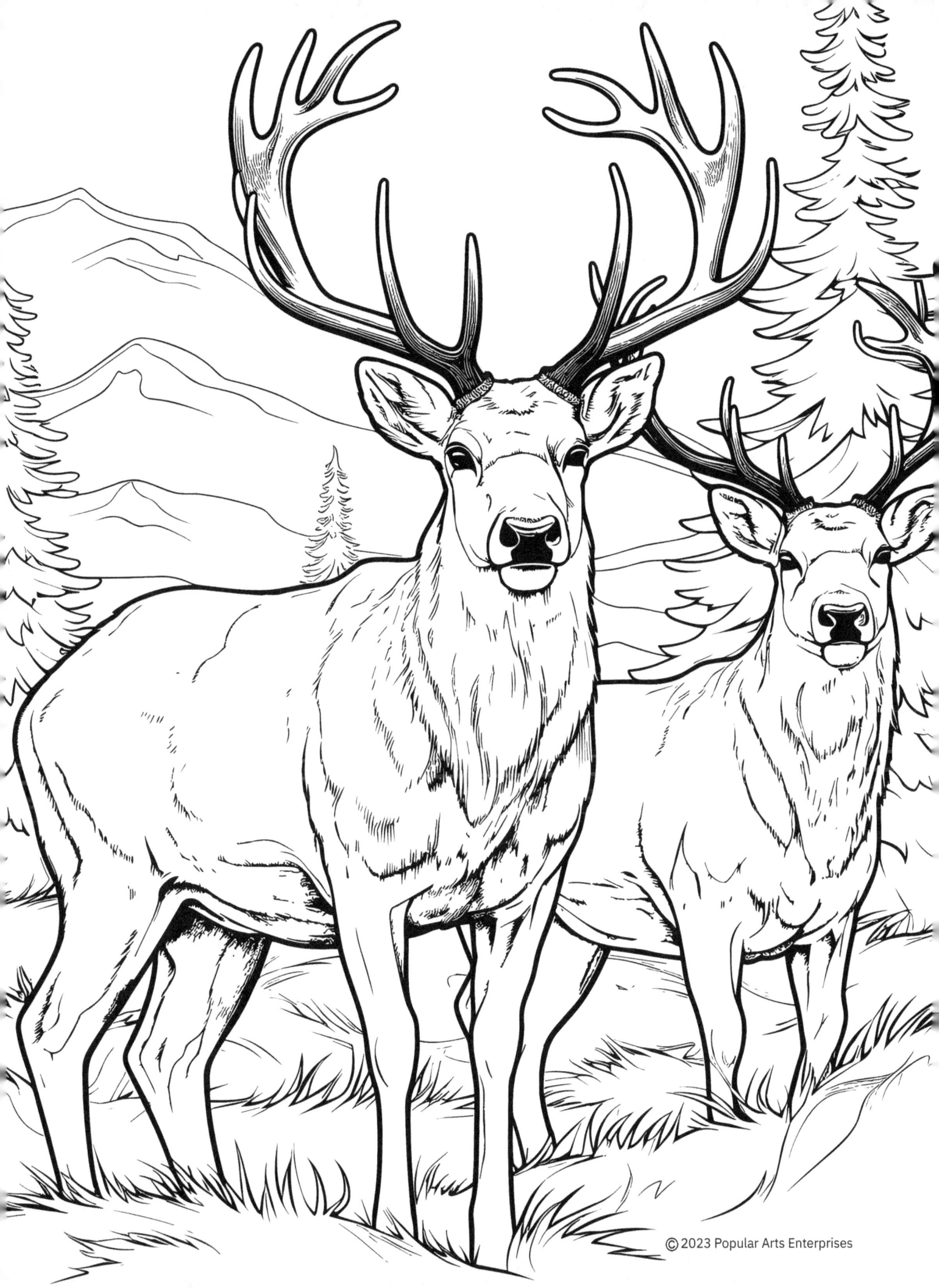

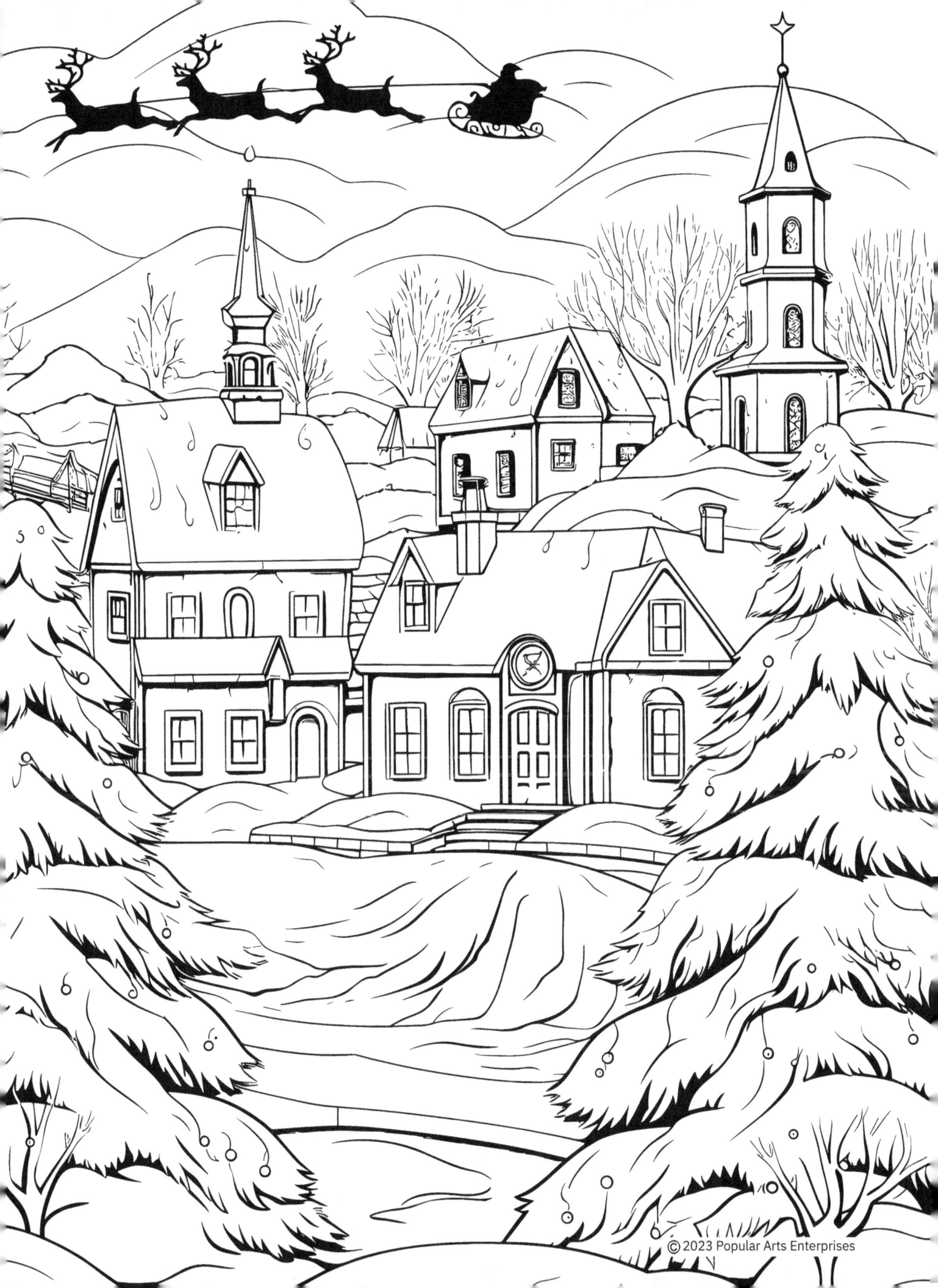

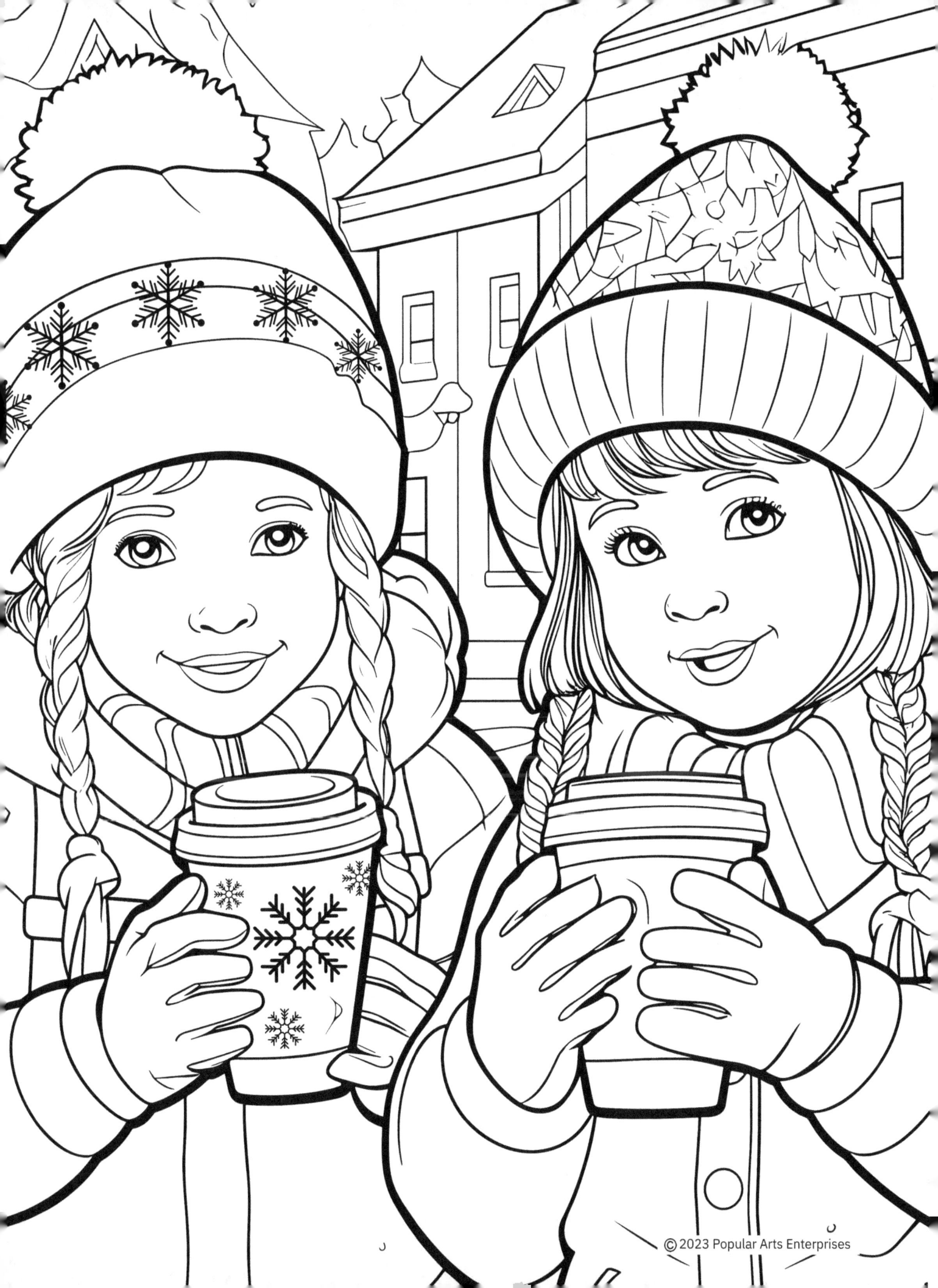

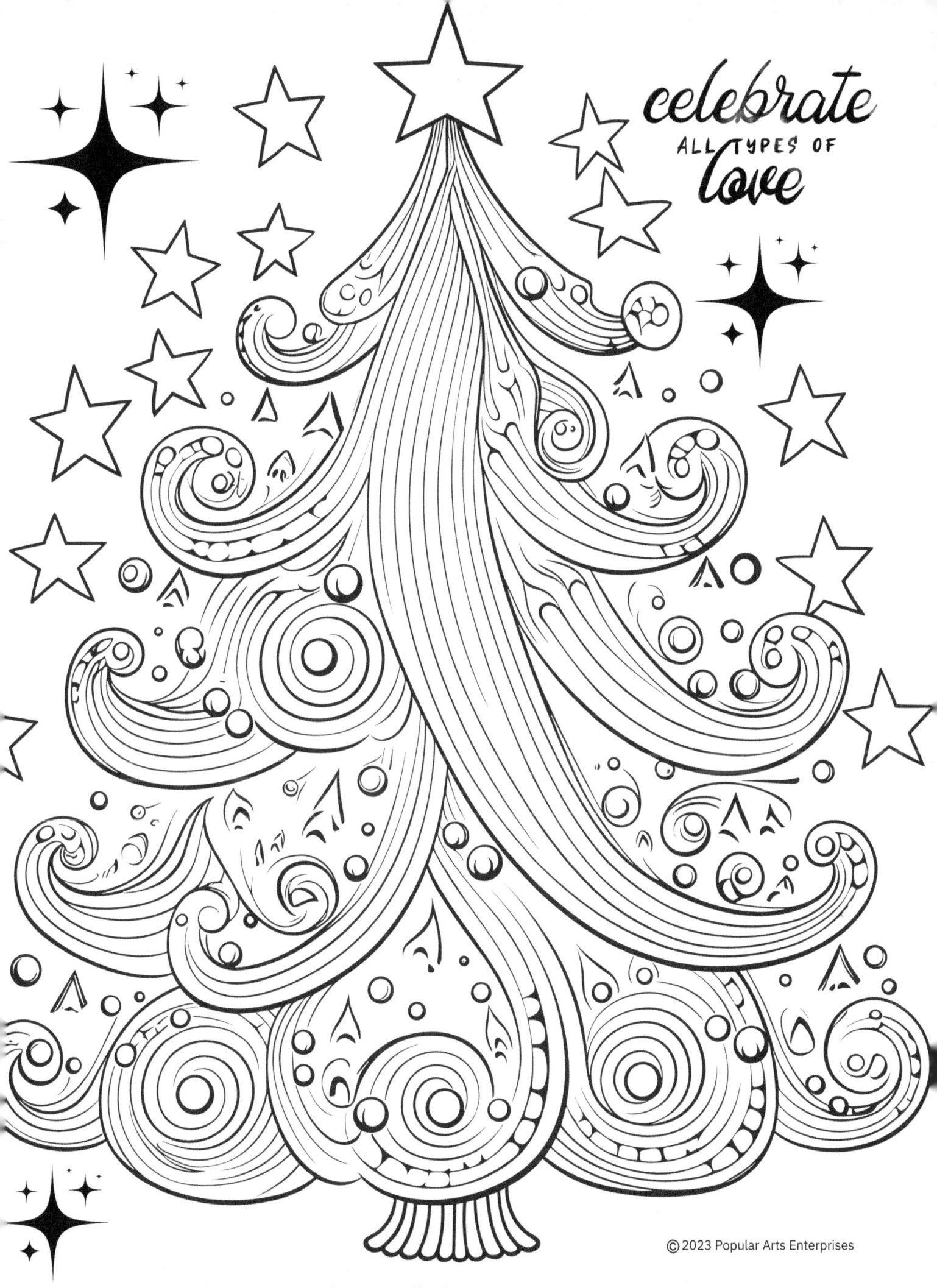

celebrate
ALL TYPES OF
love

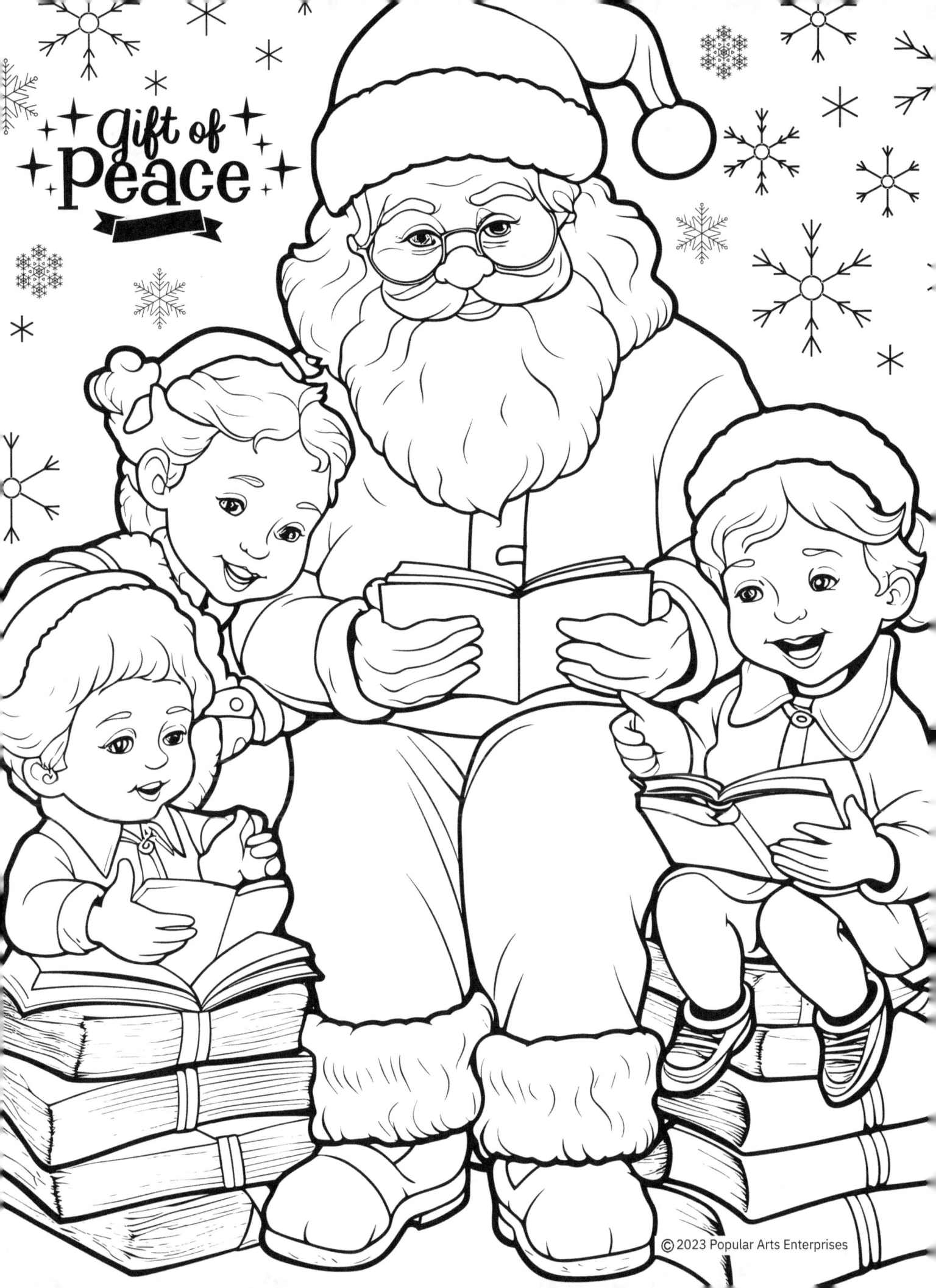

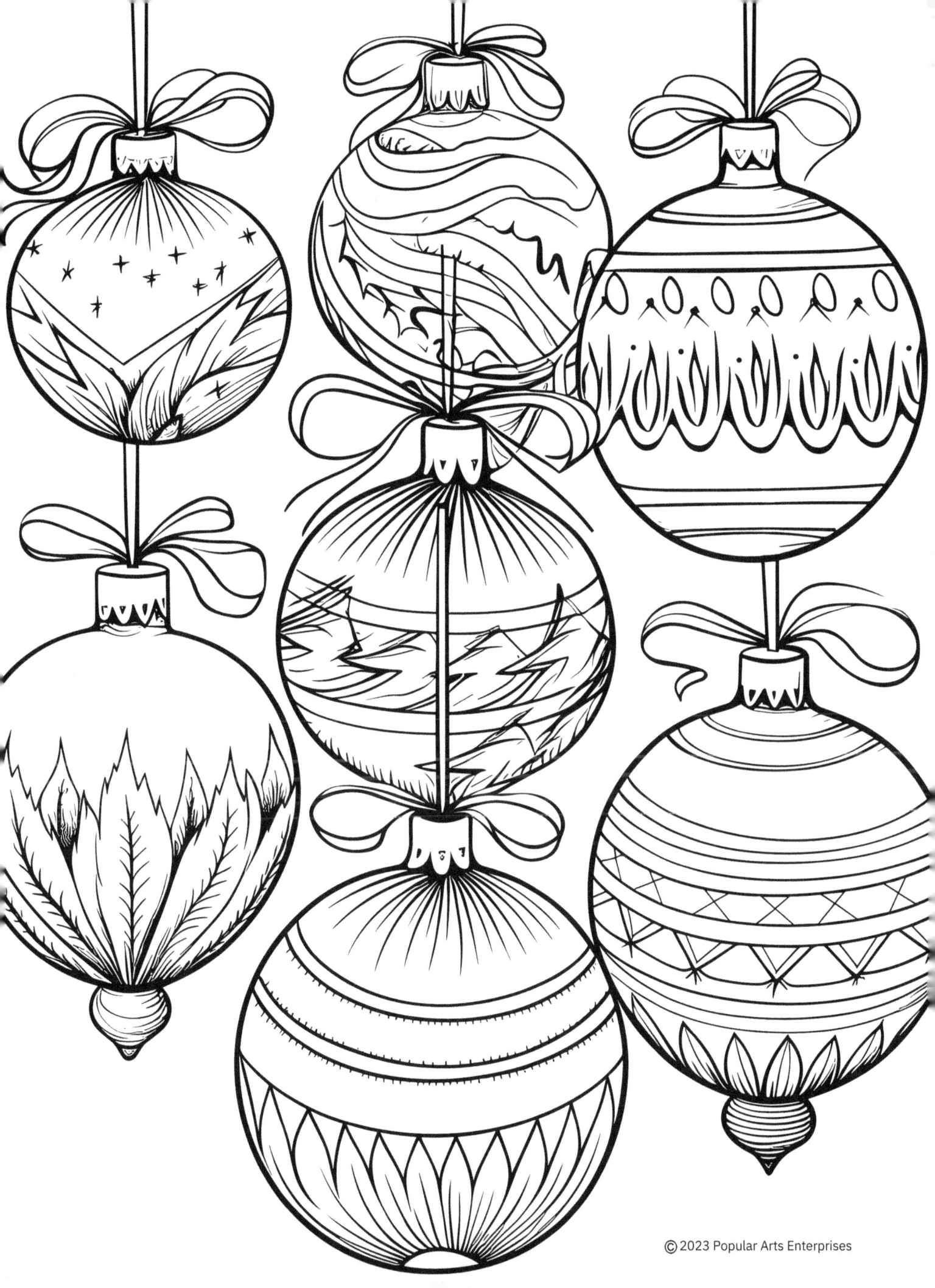

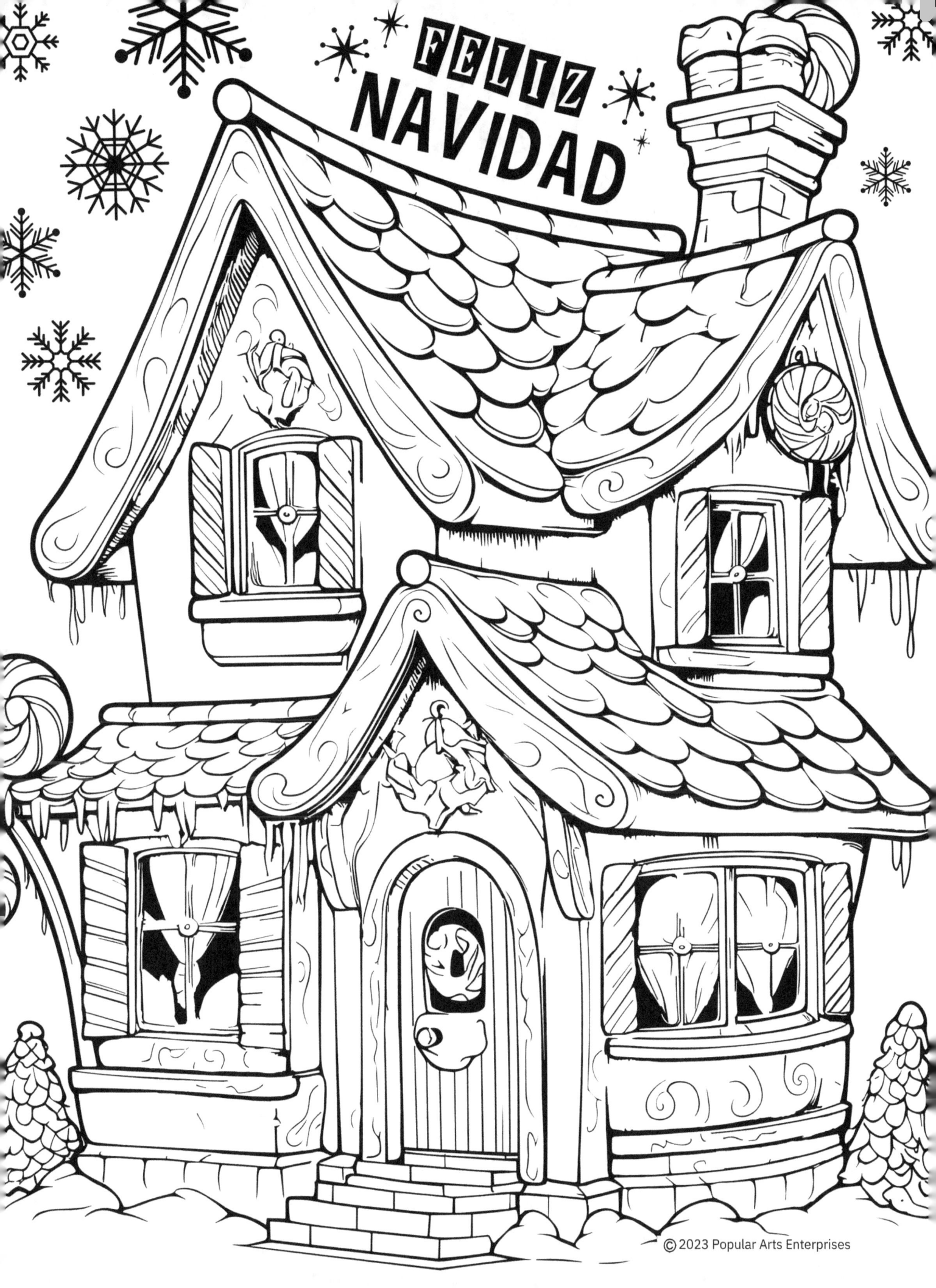

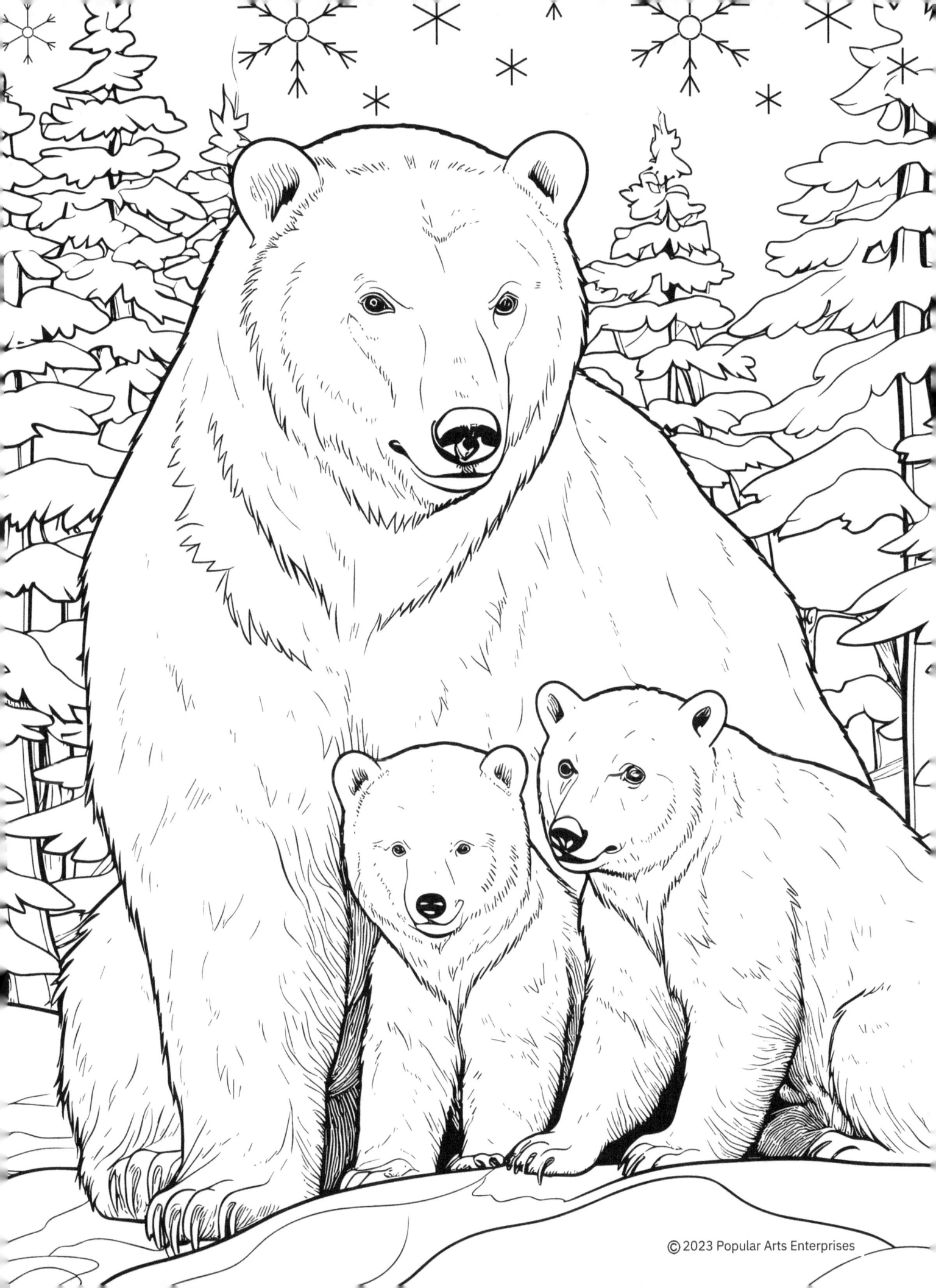

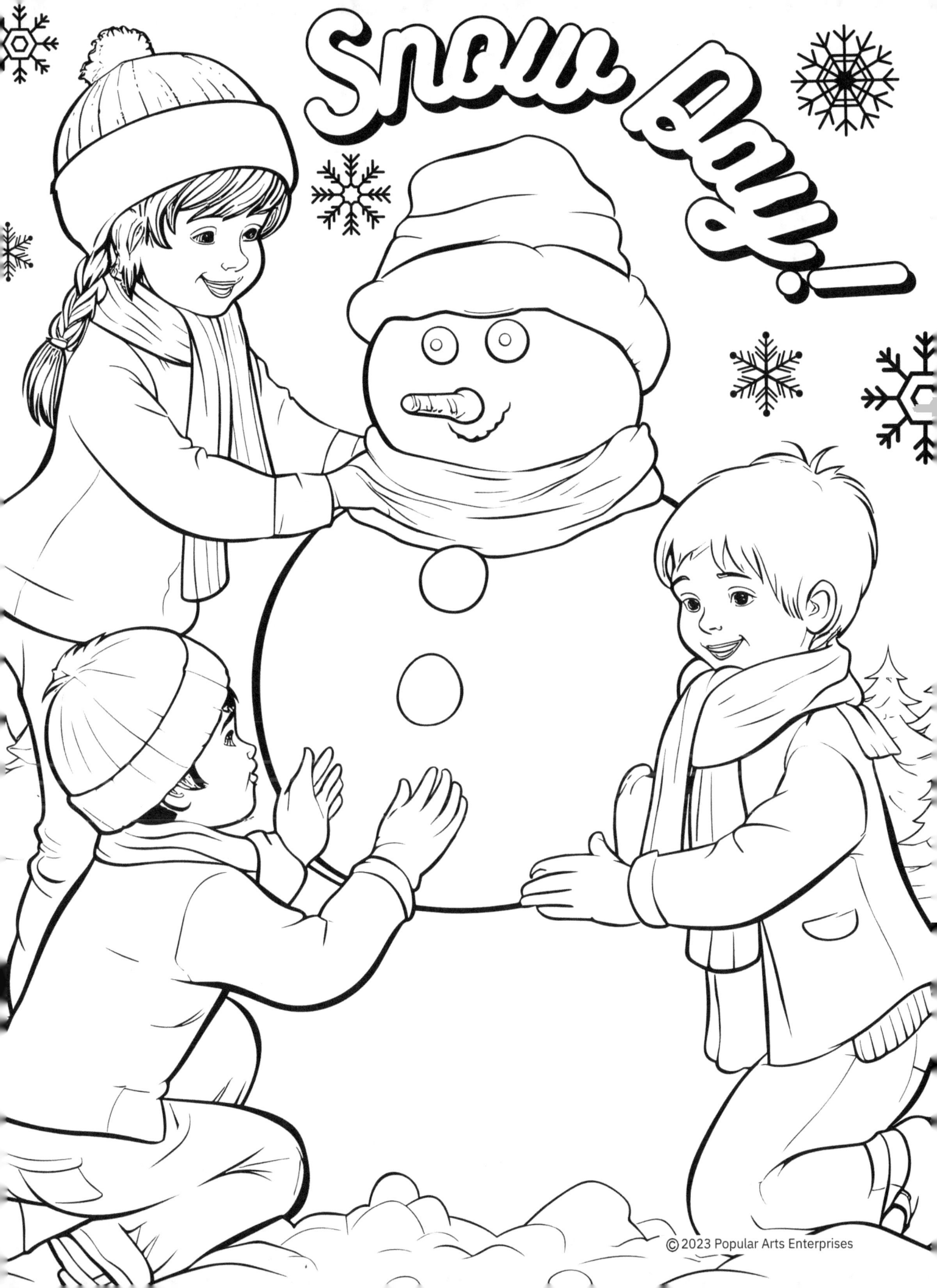

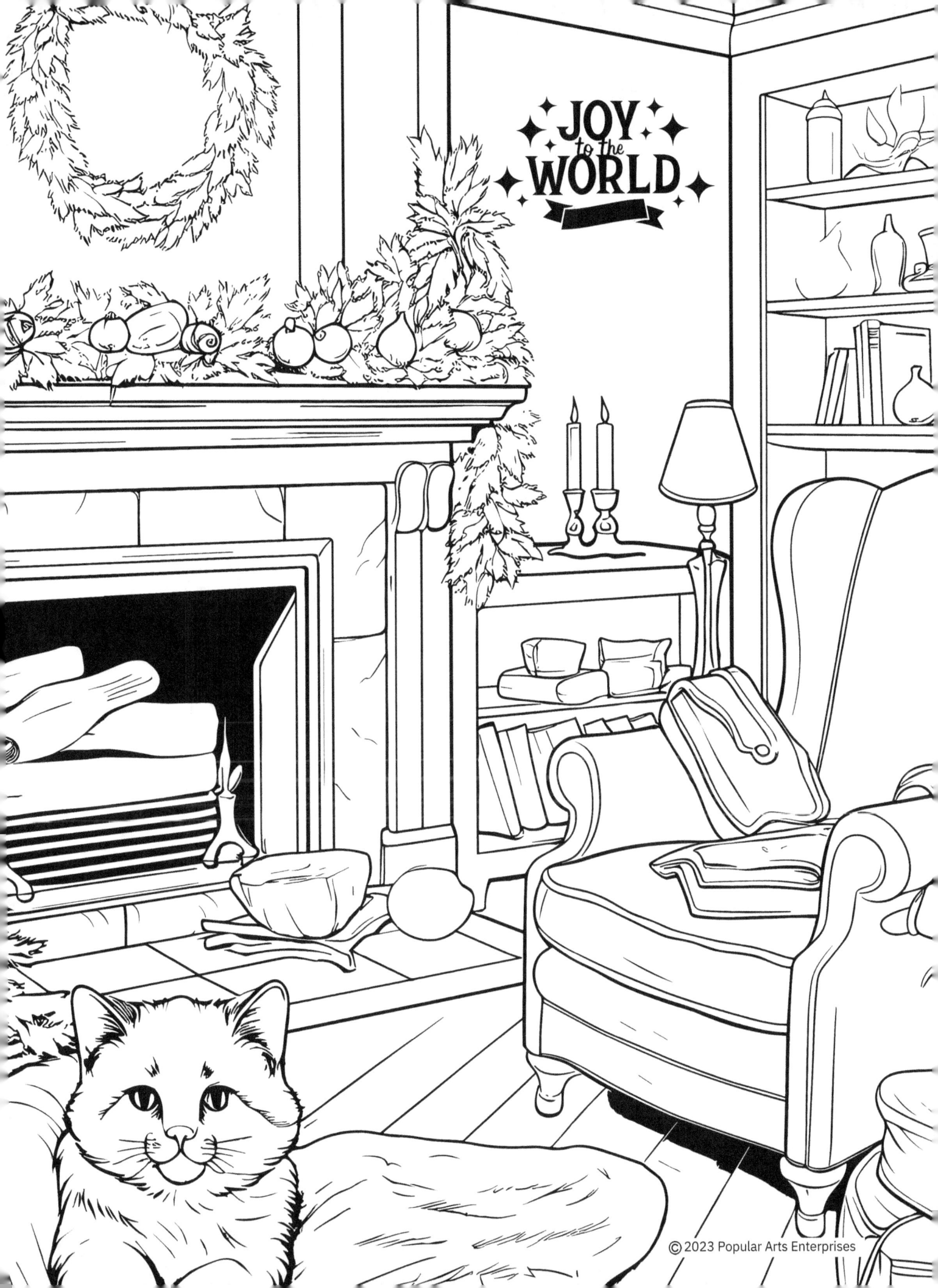

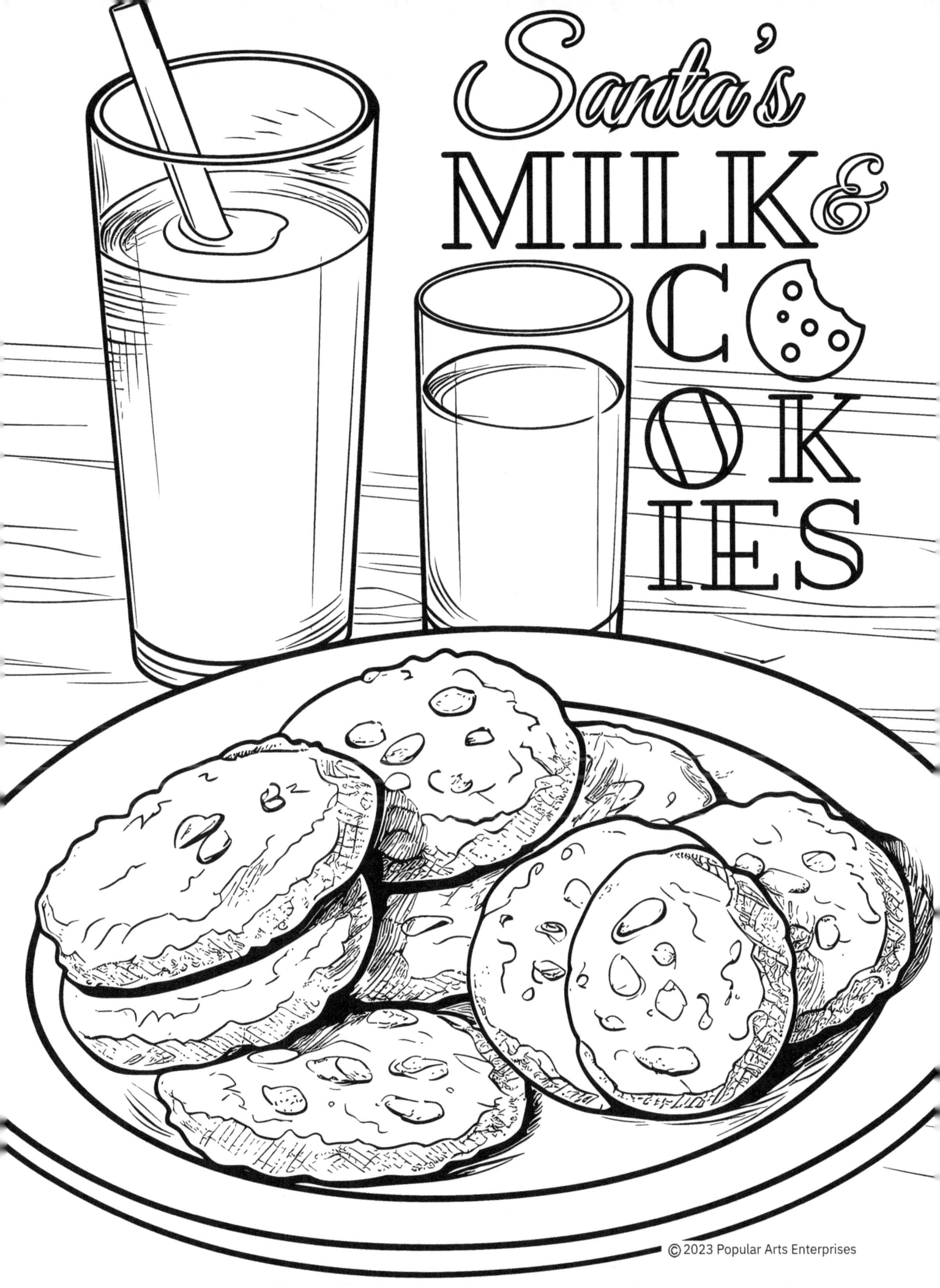

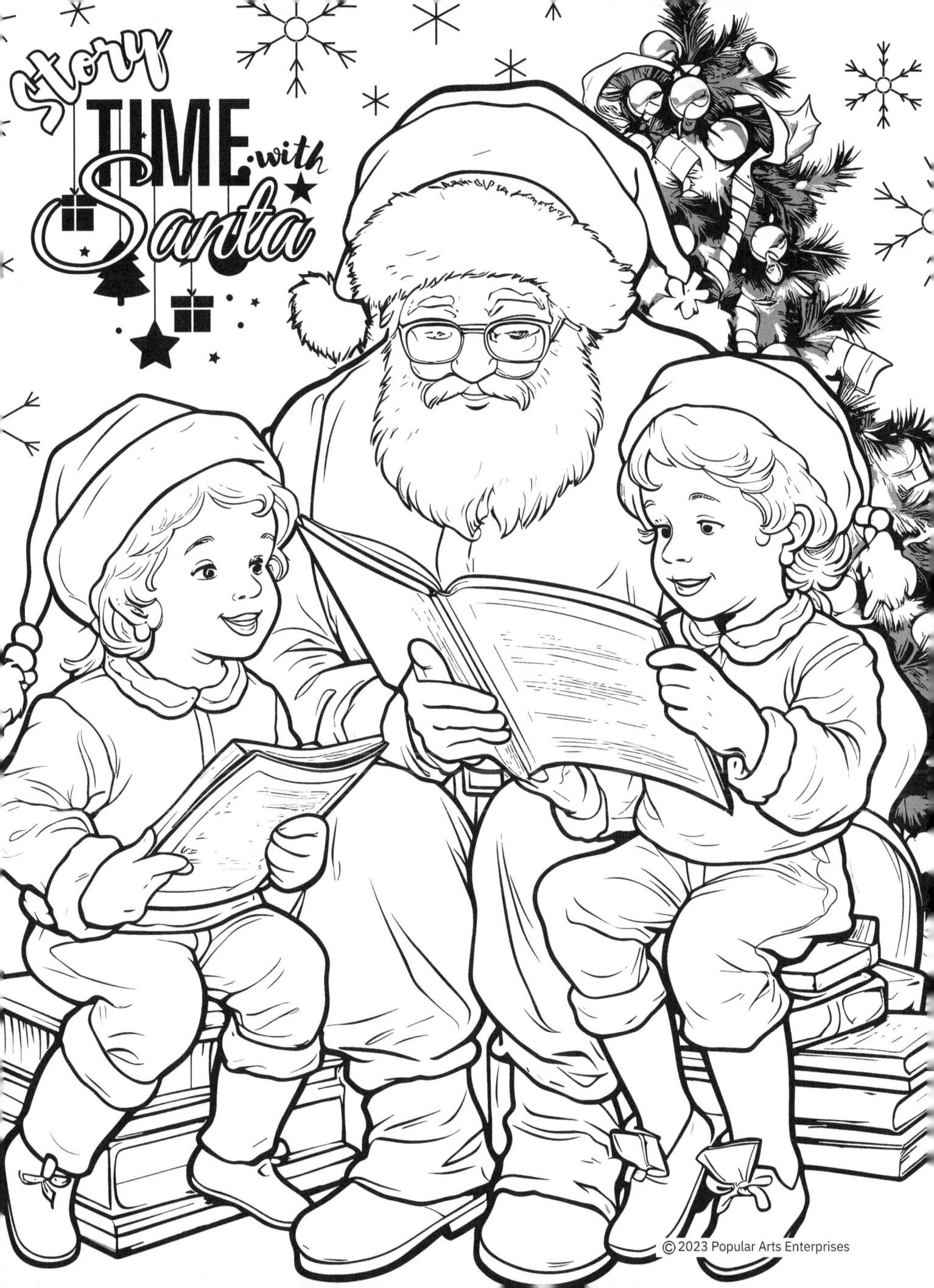

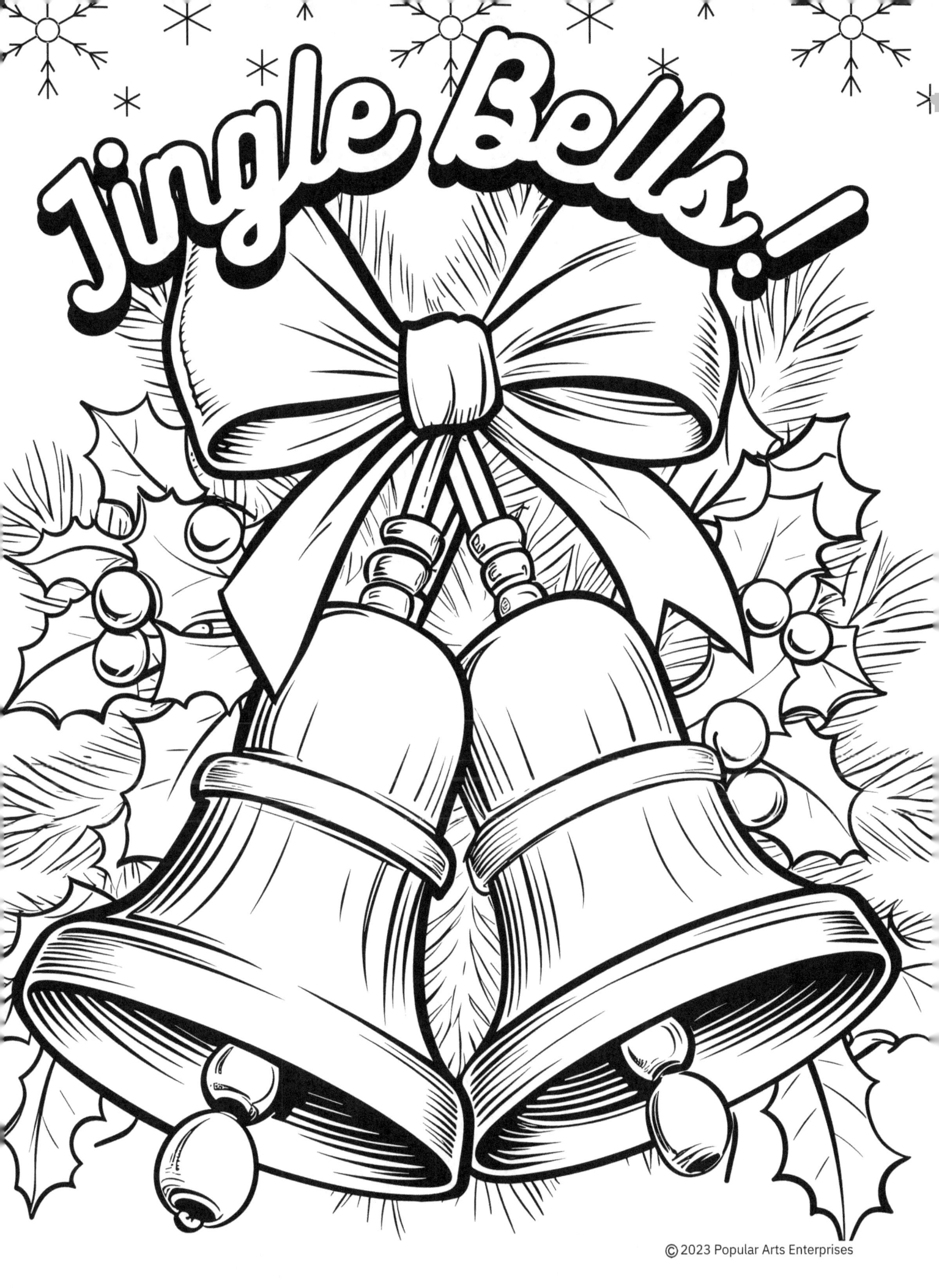

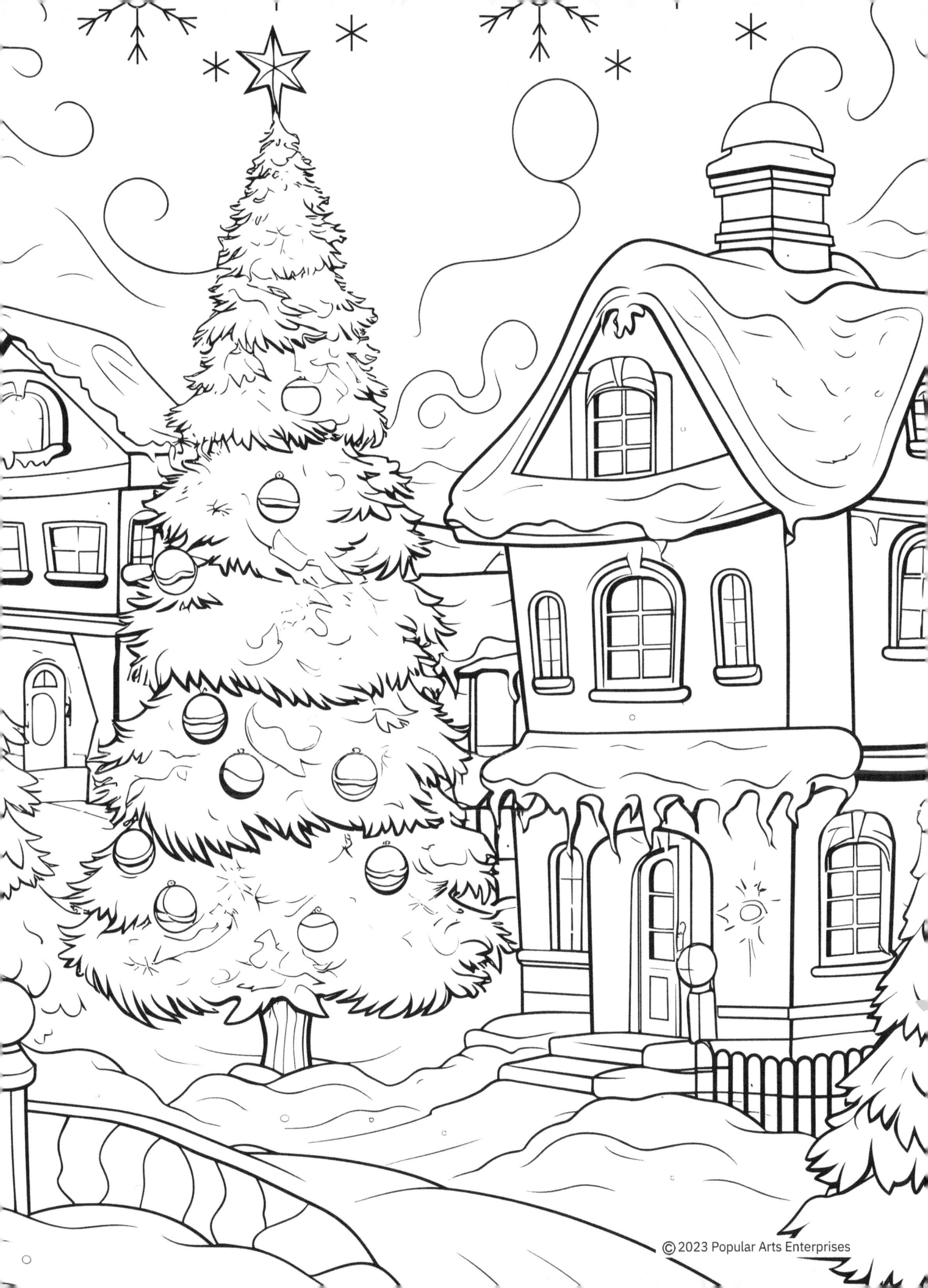

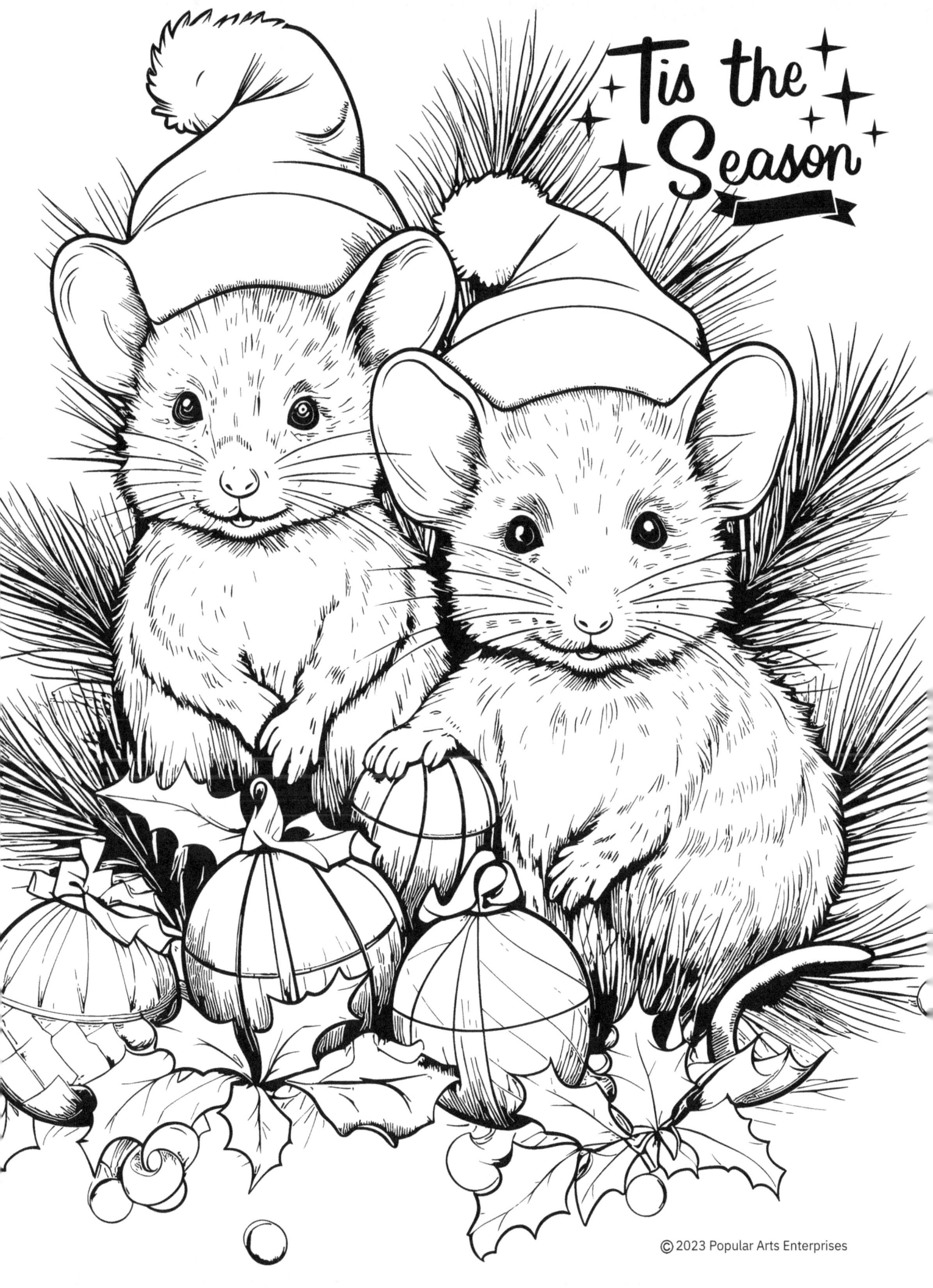

Tis the Season

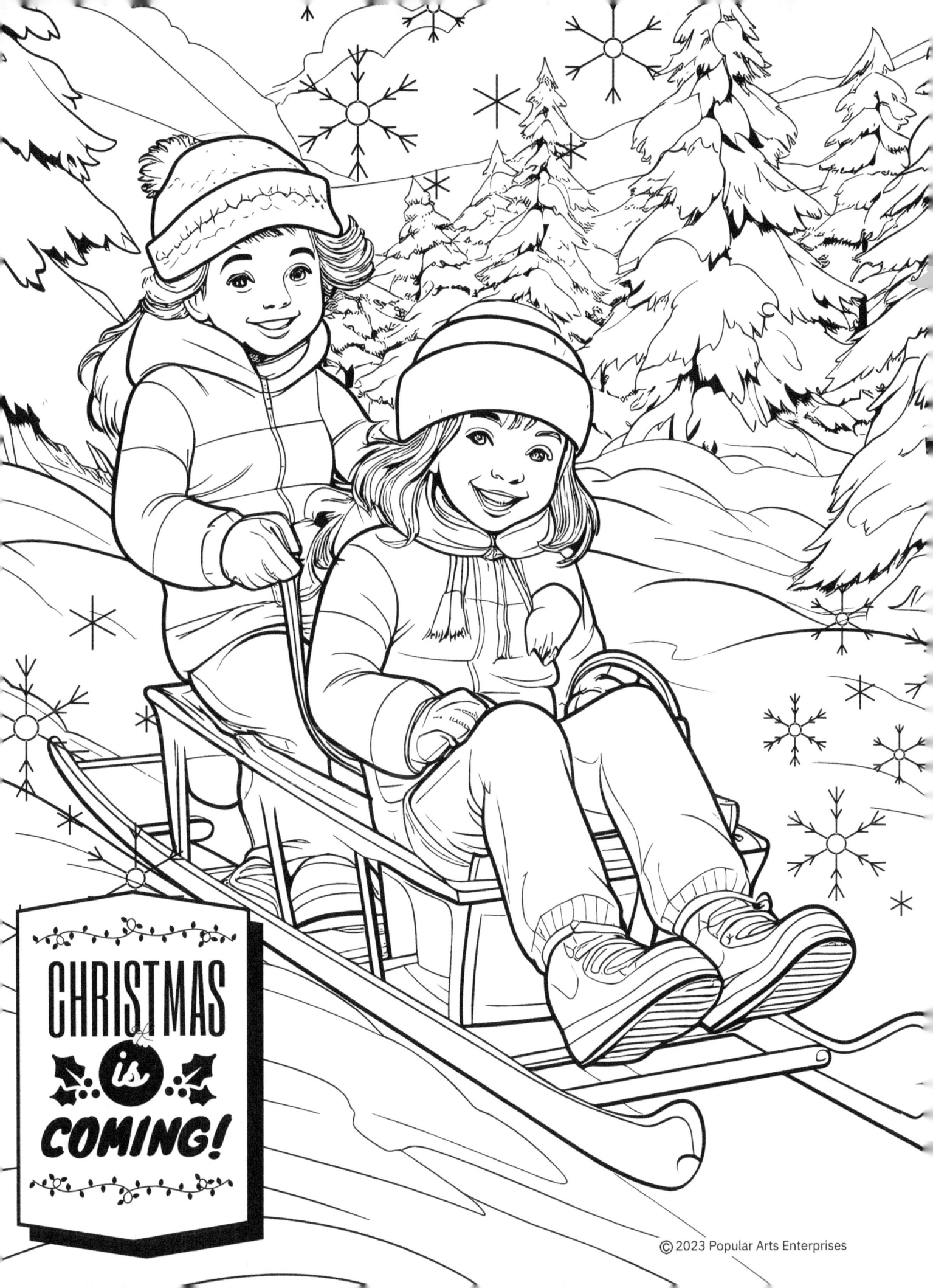

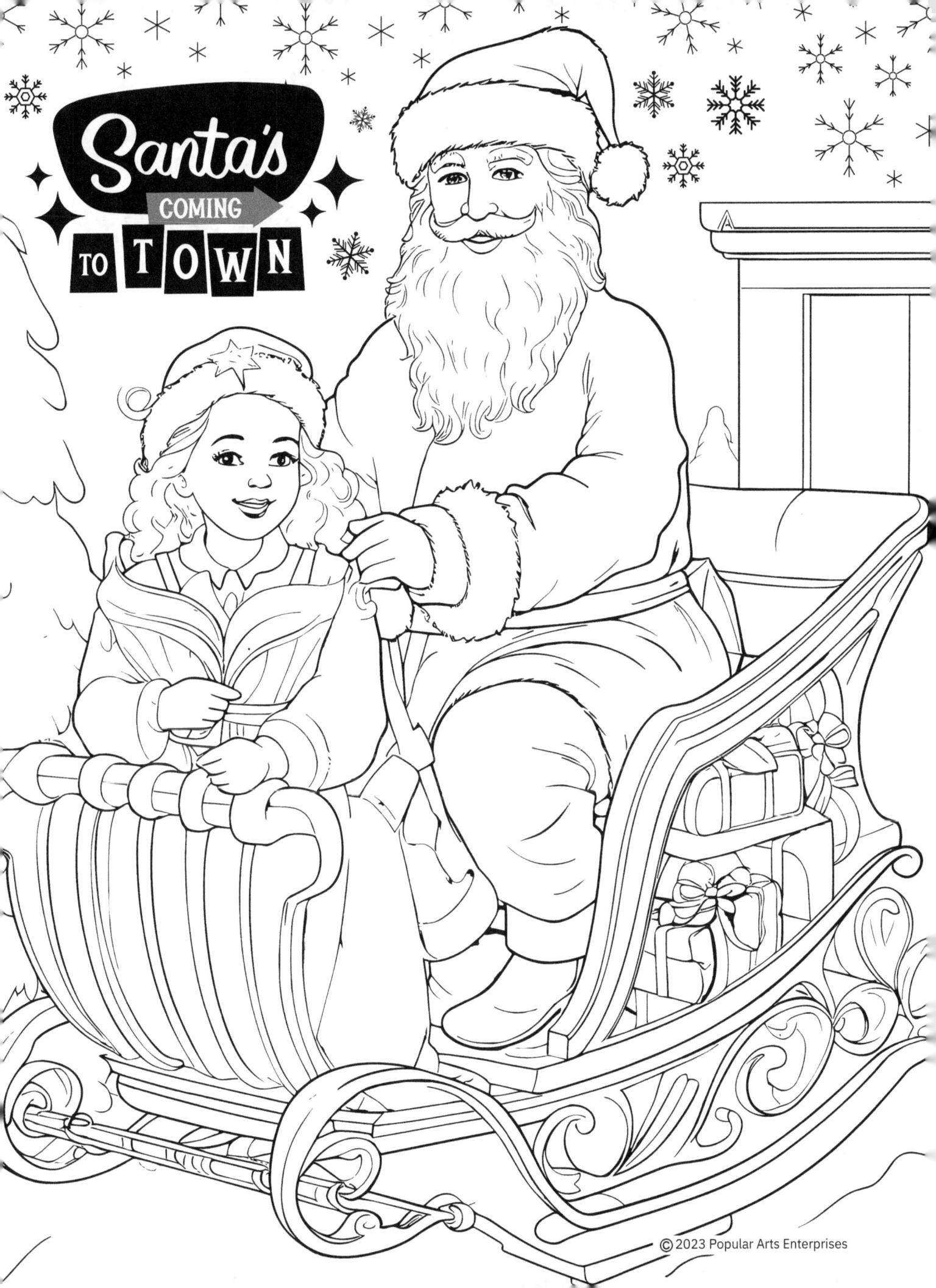

Santa's COMING TO TOWN

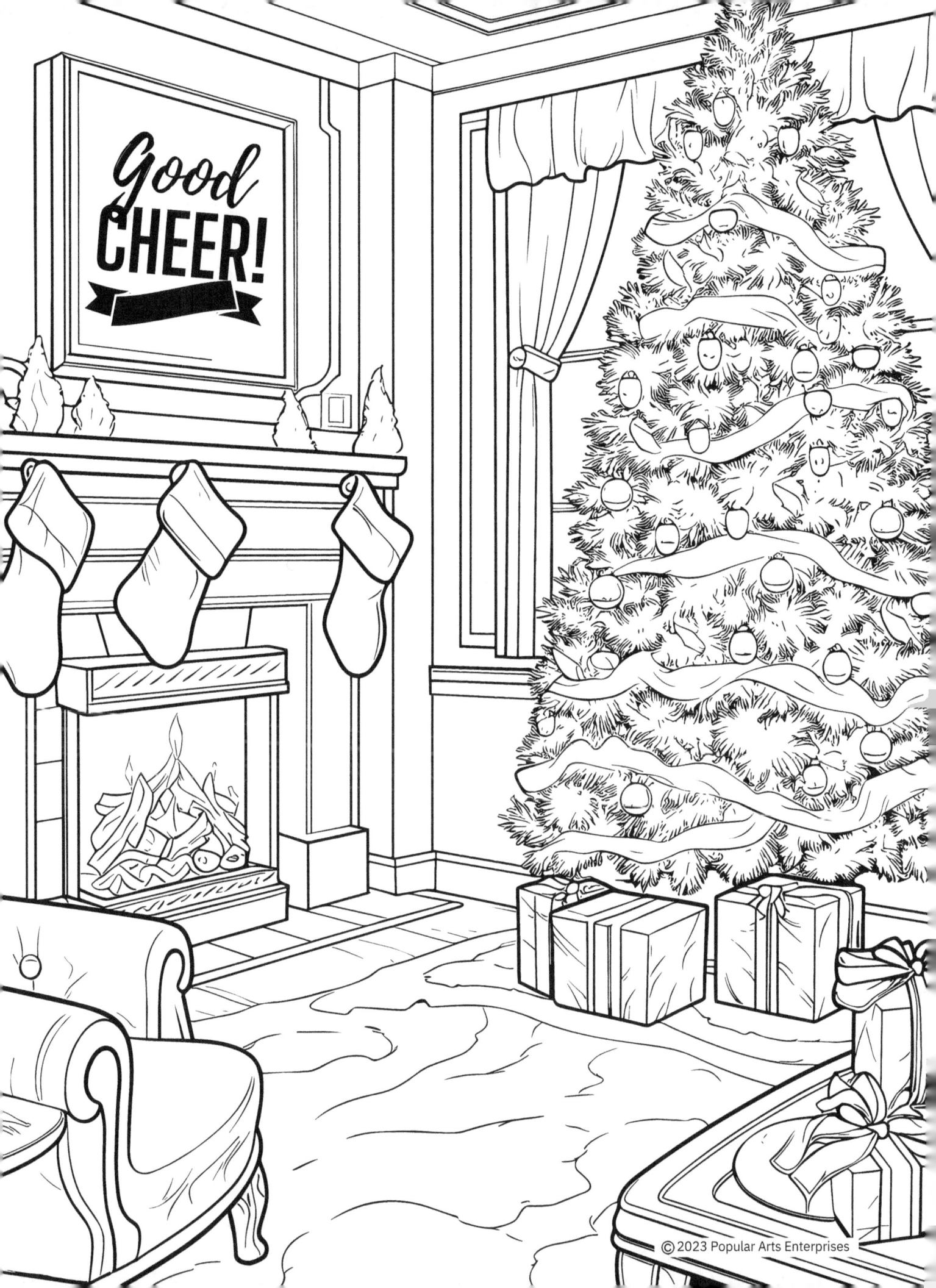

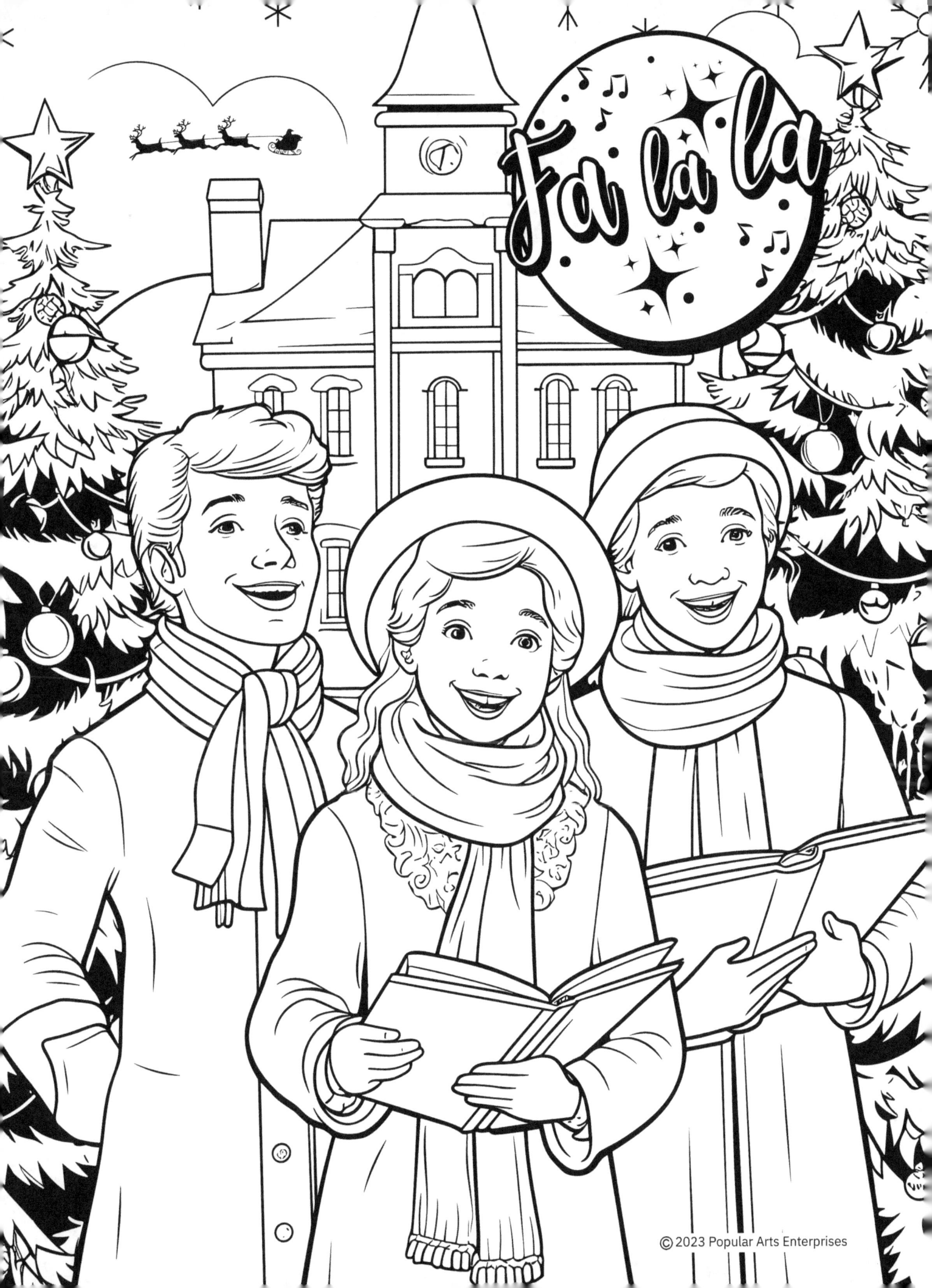

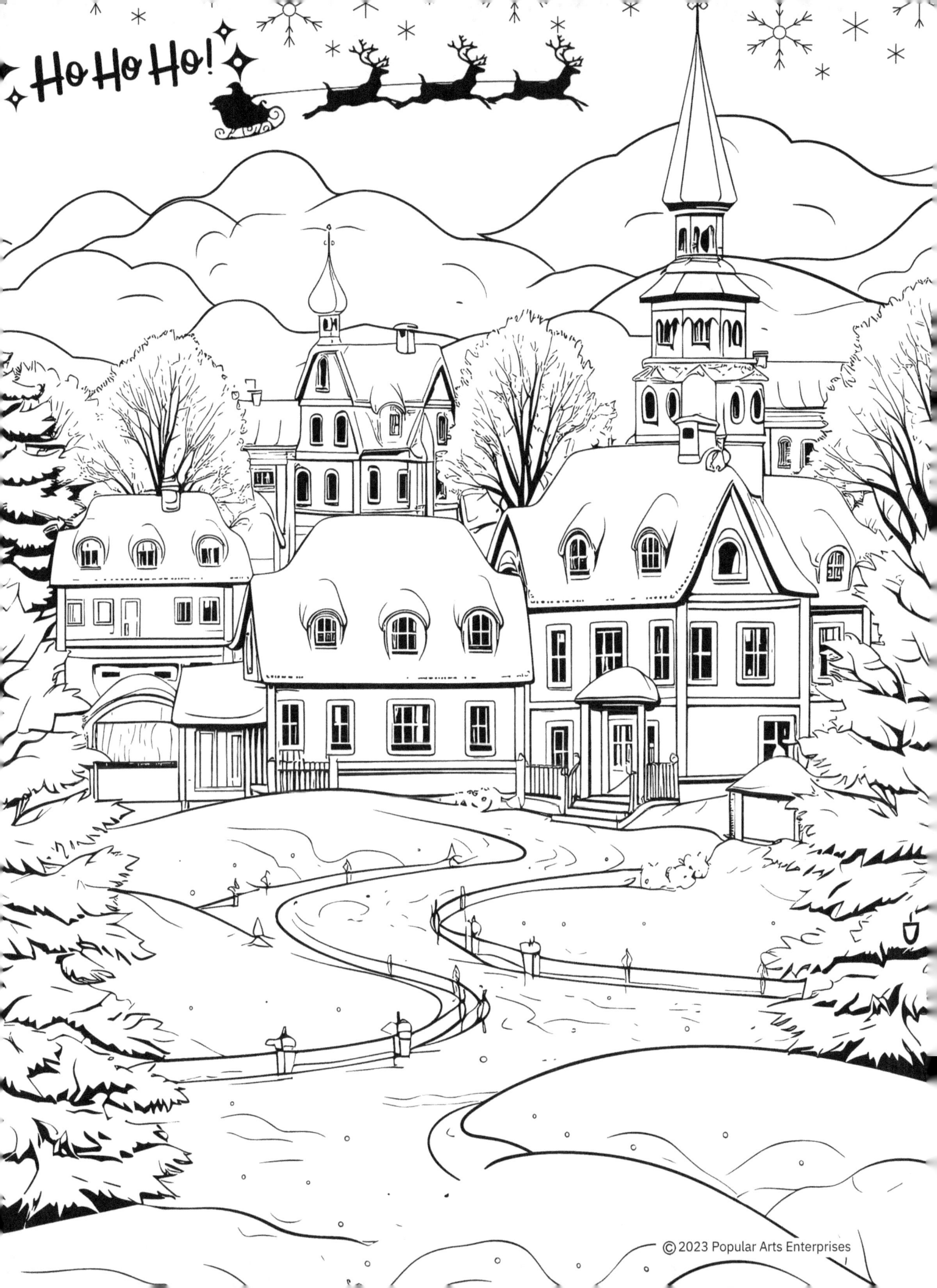

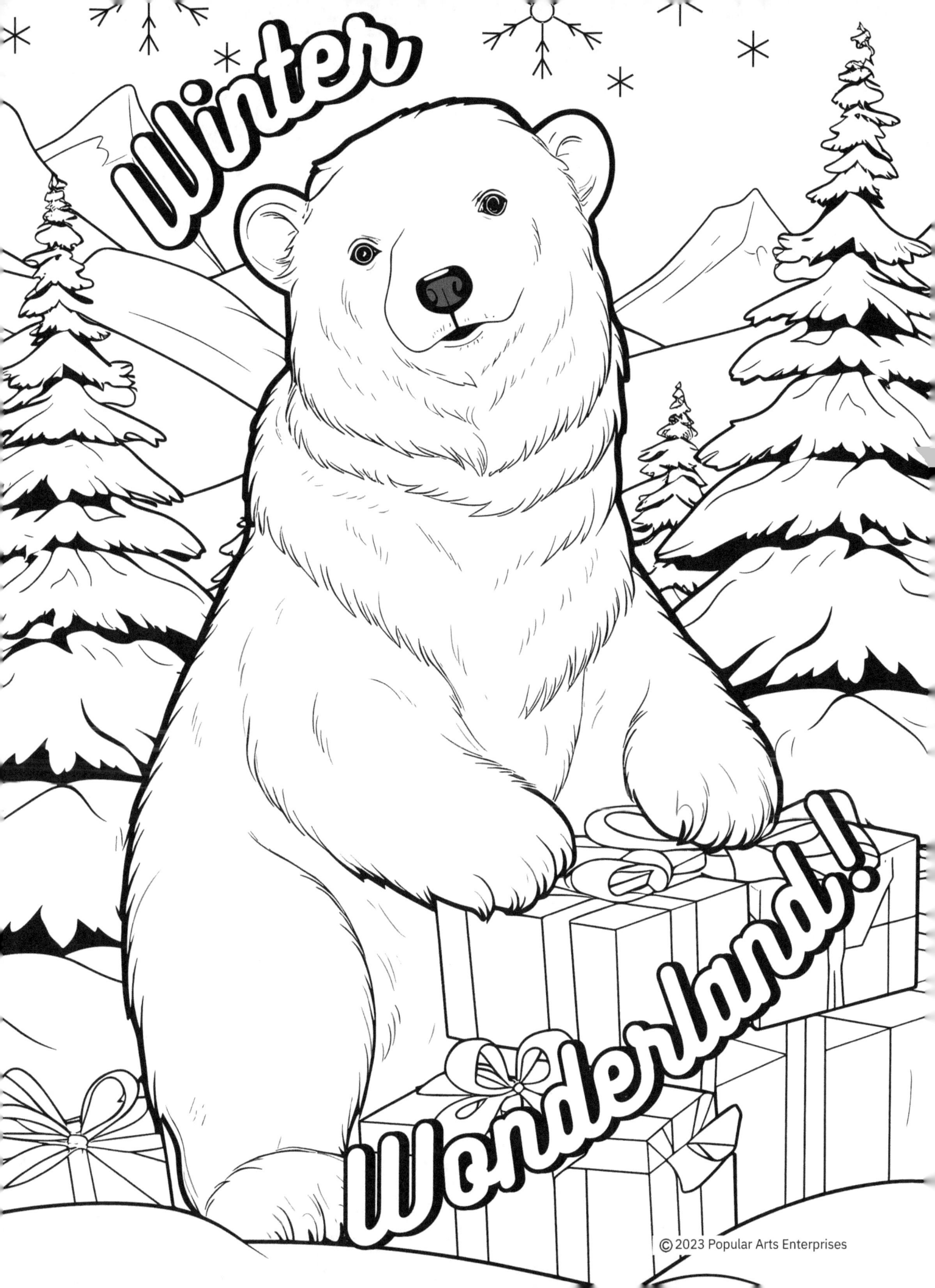

Winter Wonderland!

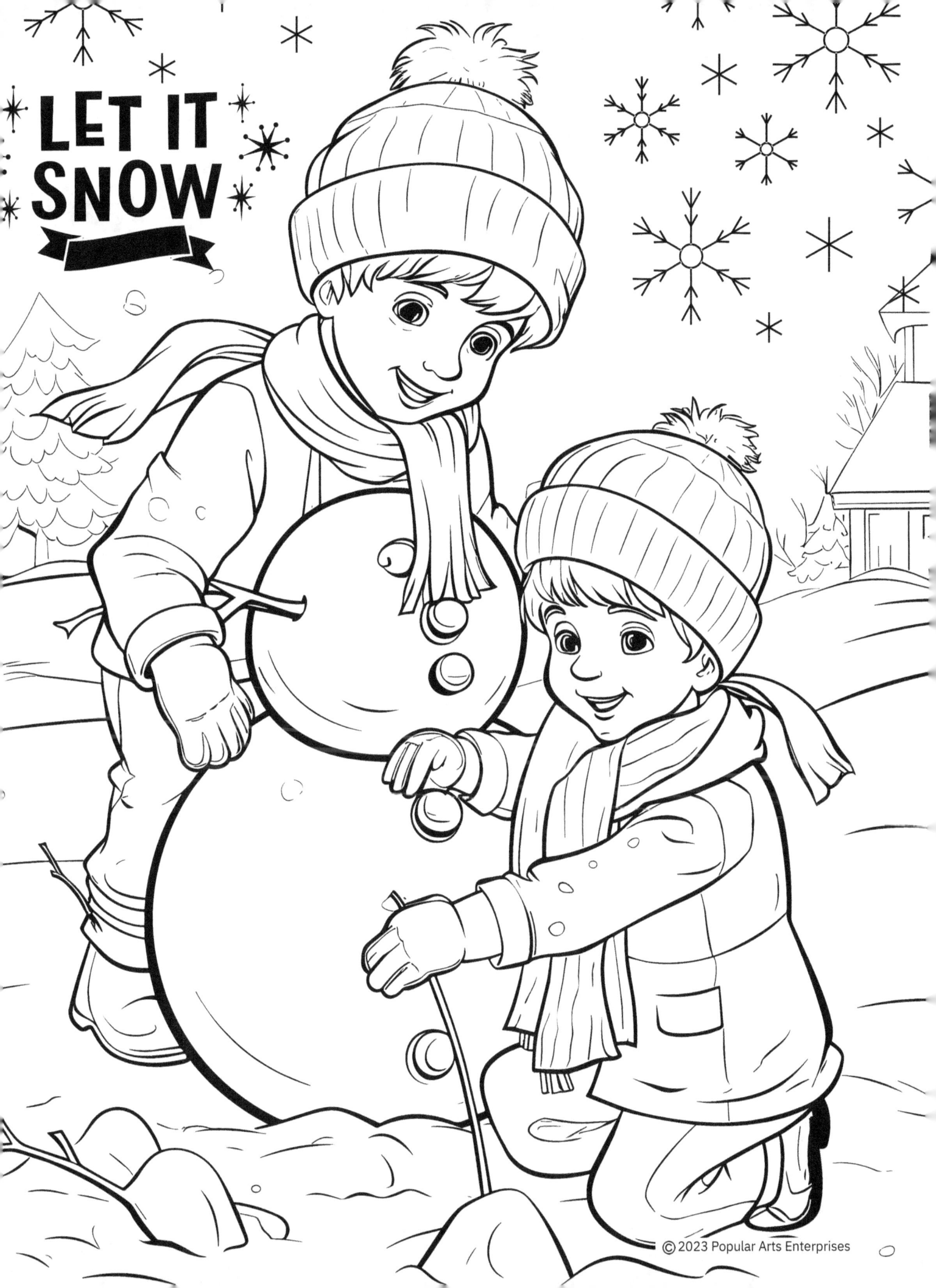

LET IT SNOW

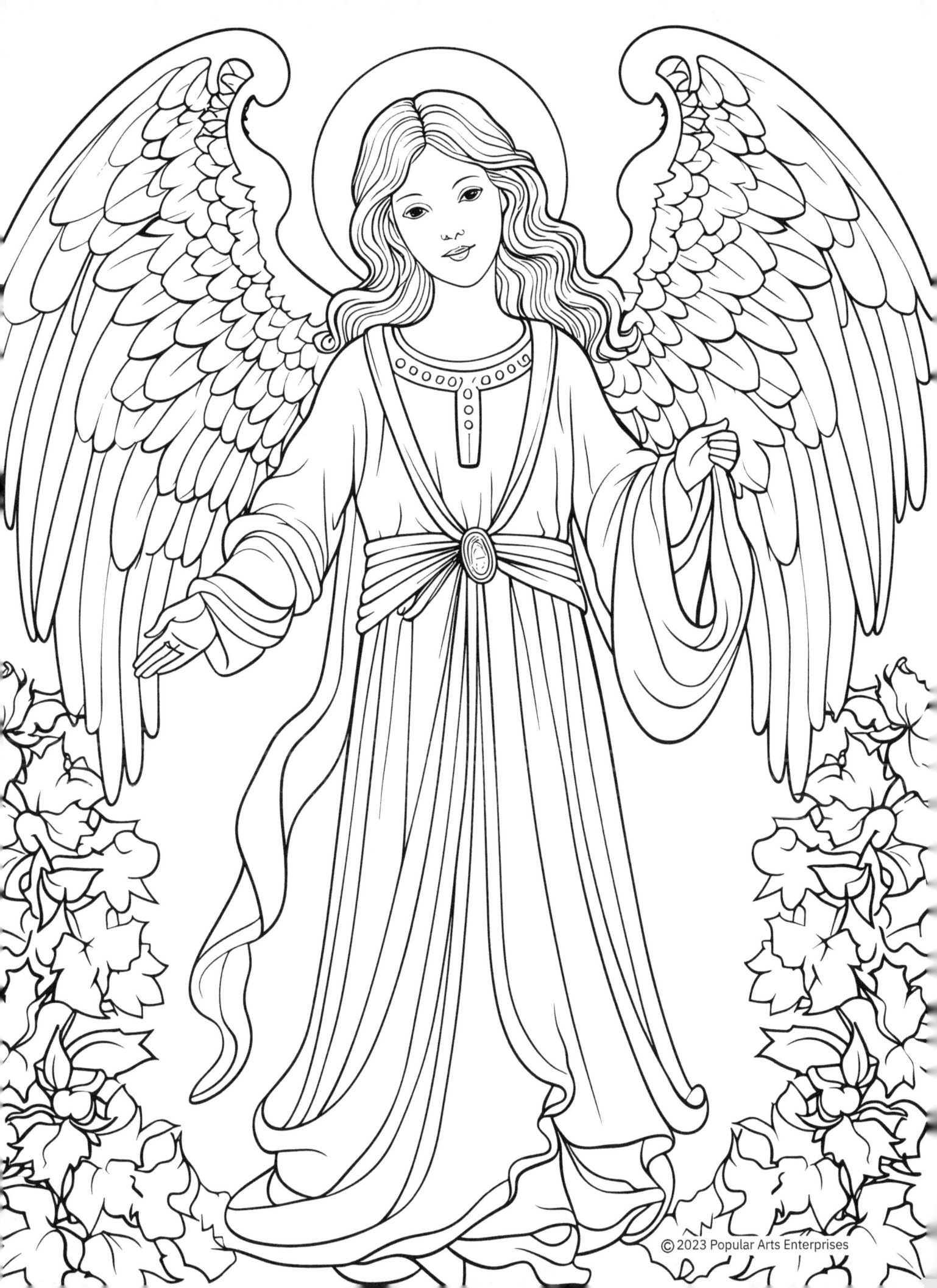

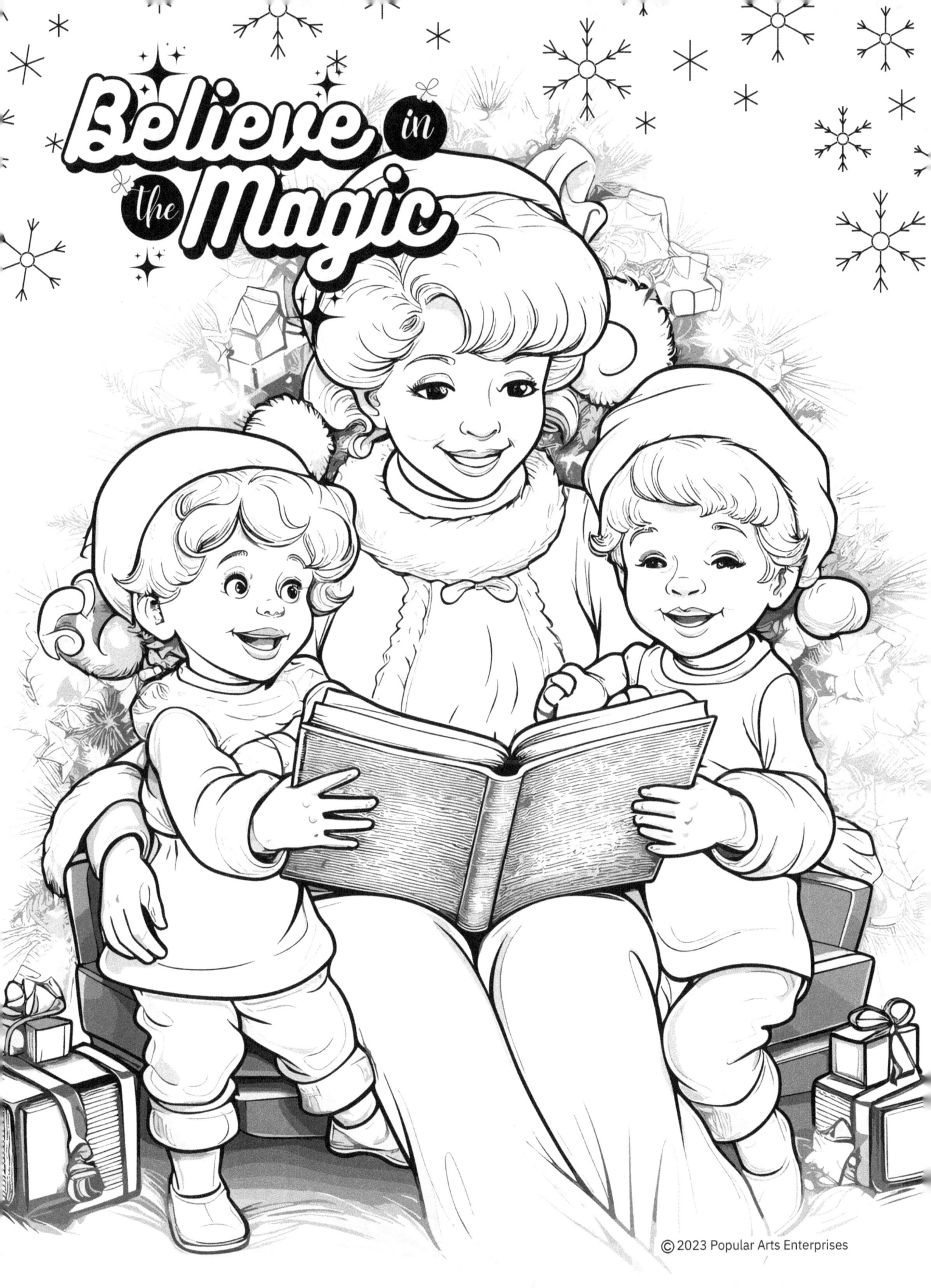

Believe in the Magic

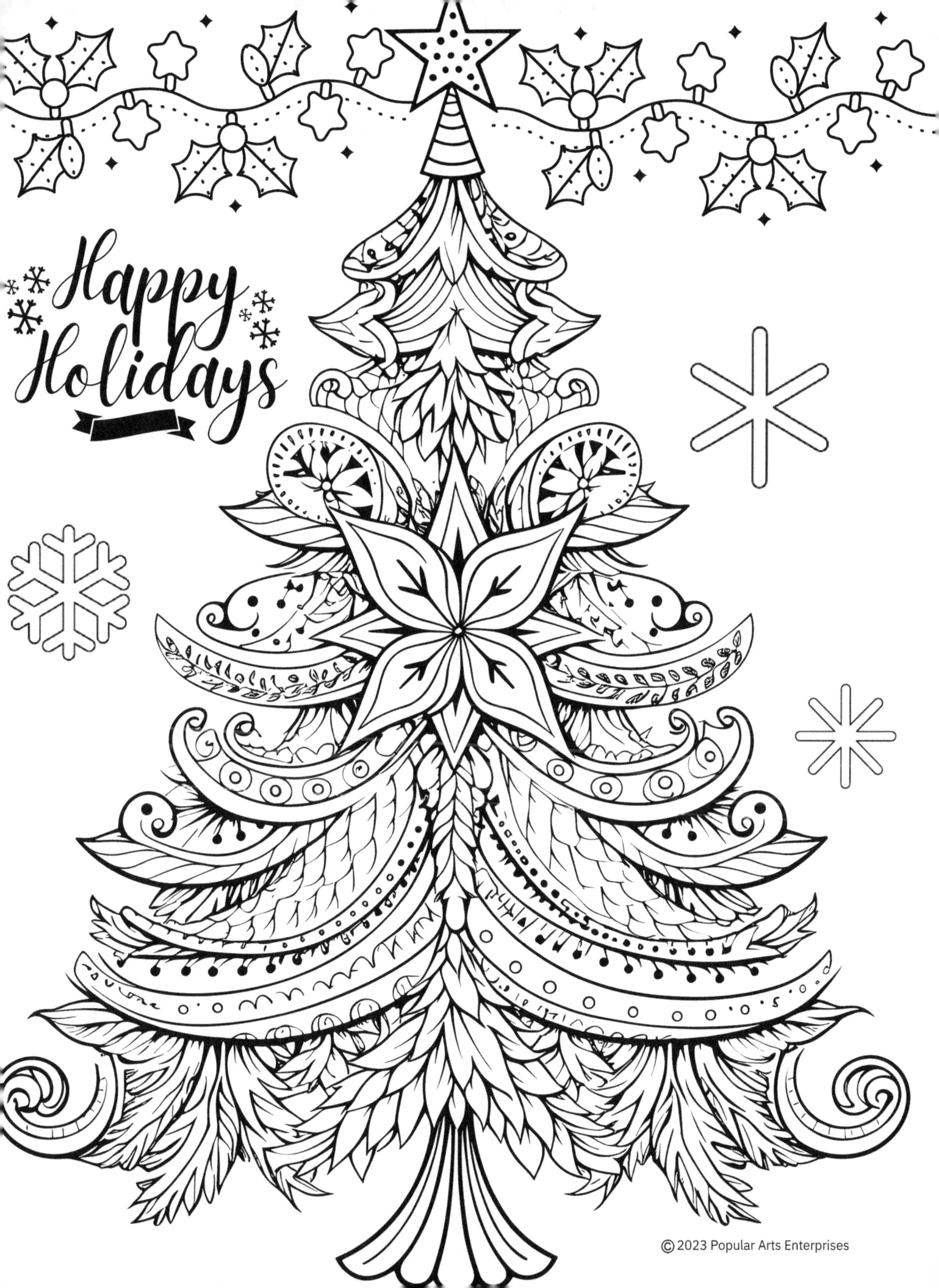

Happy Holidays

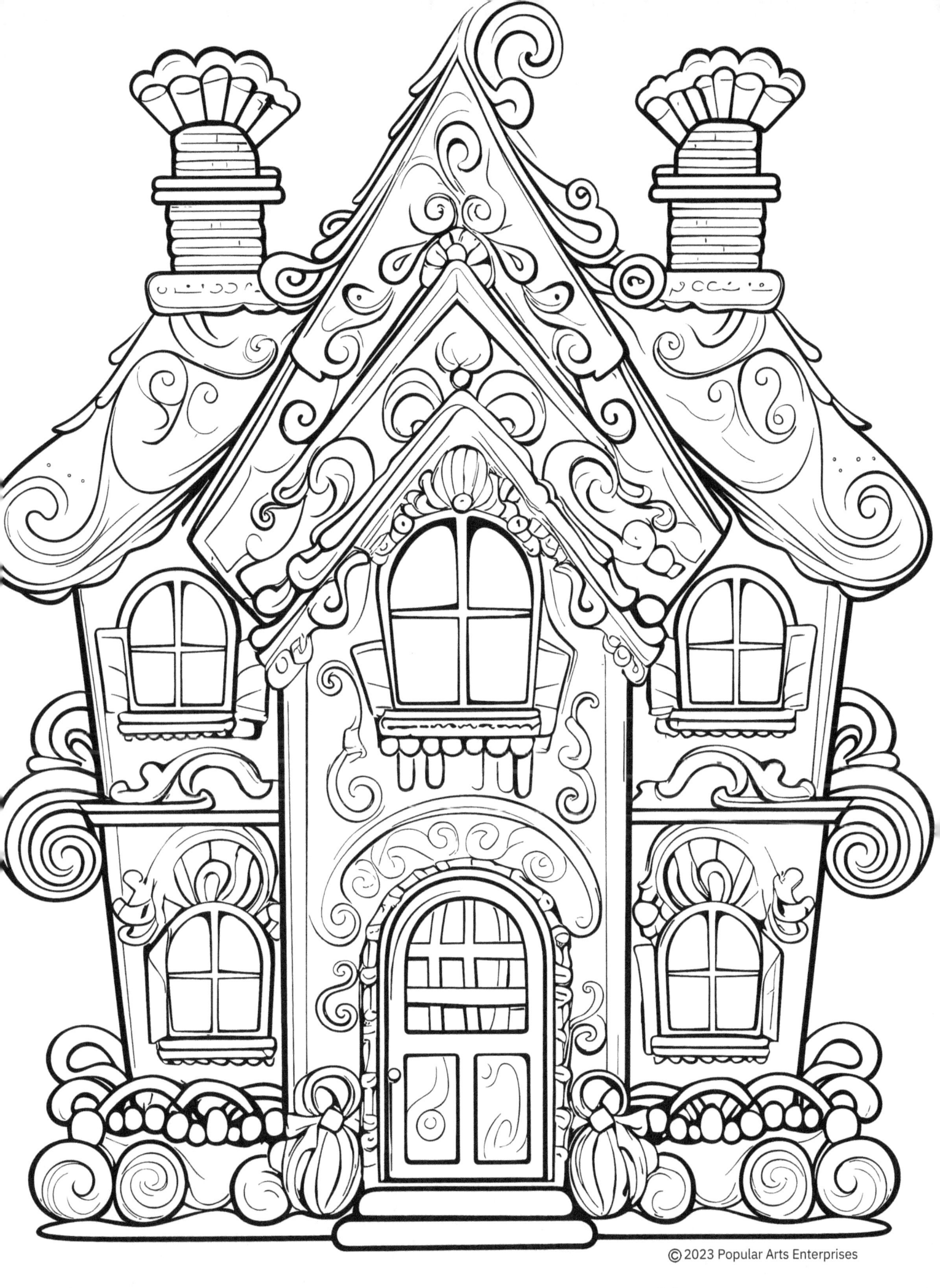

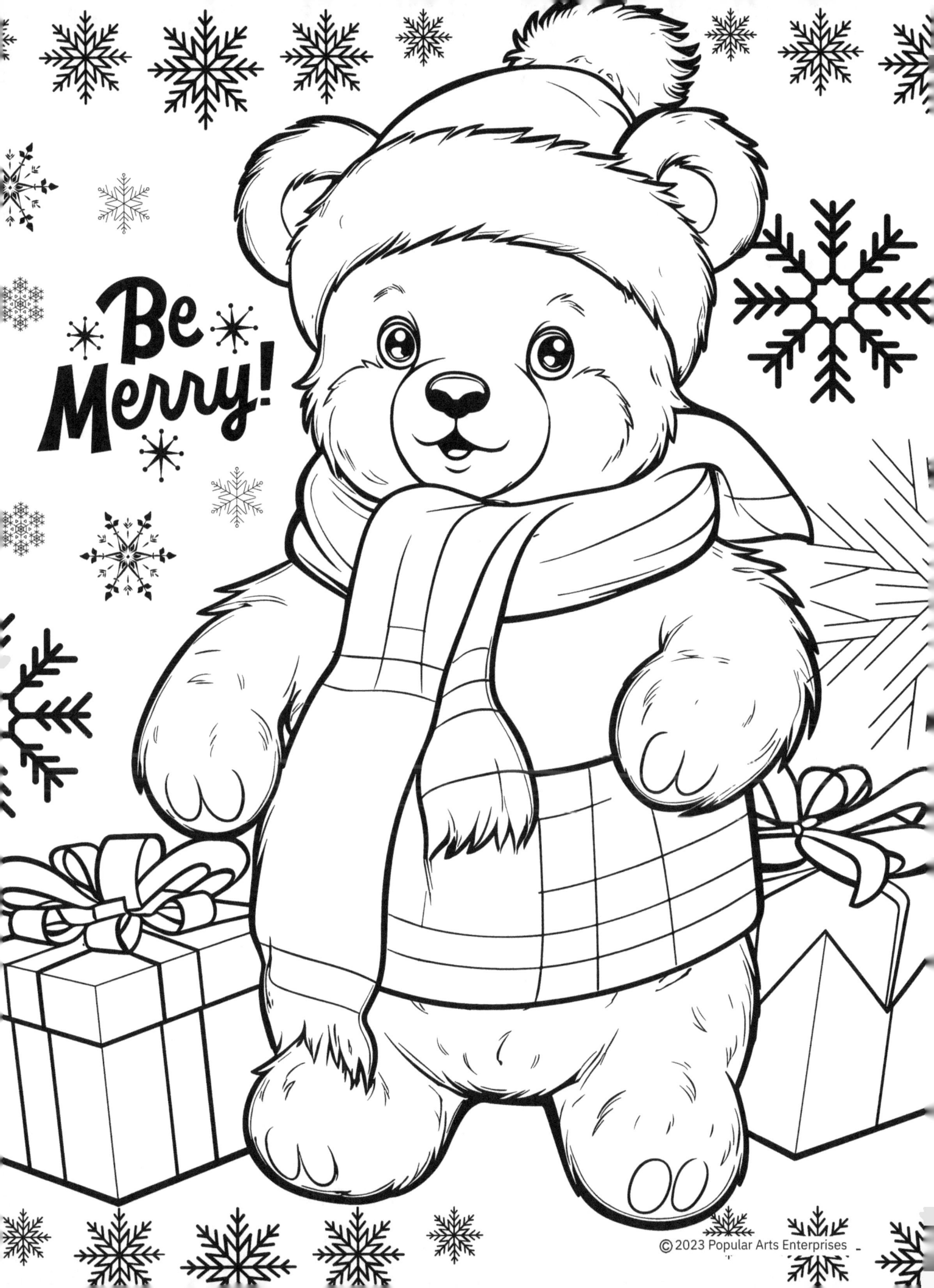

Be Merry!

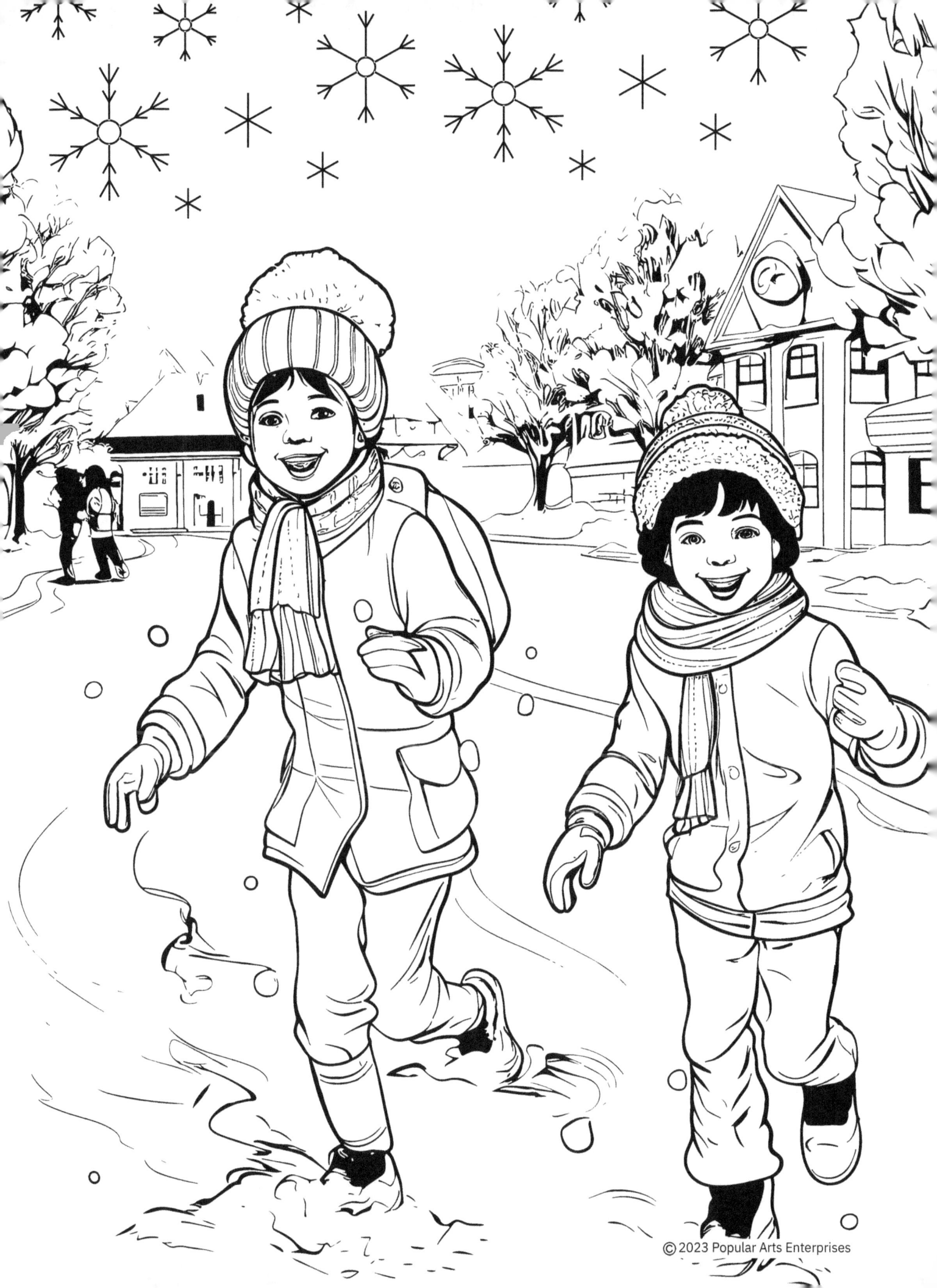

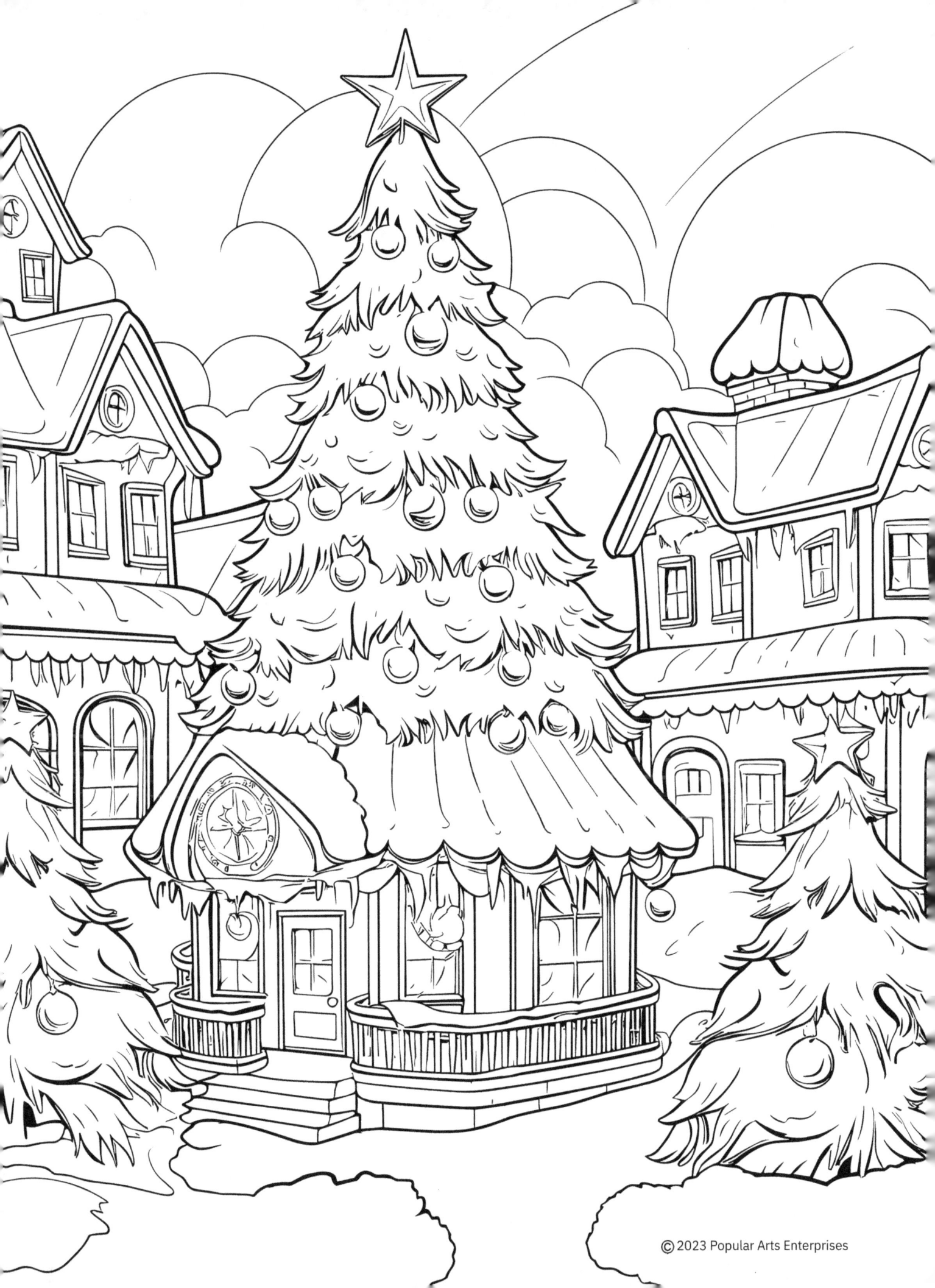

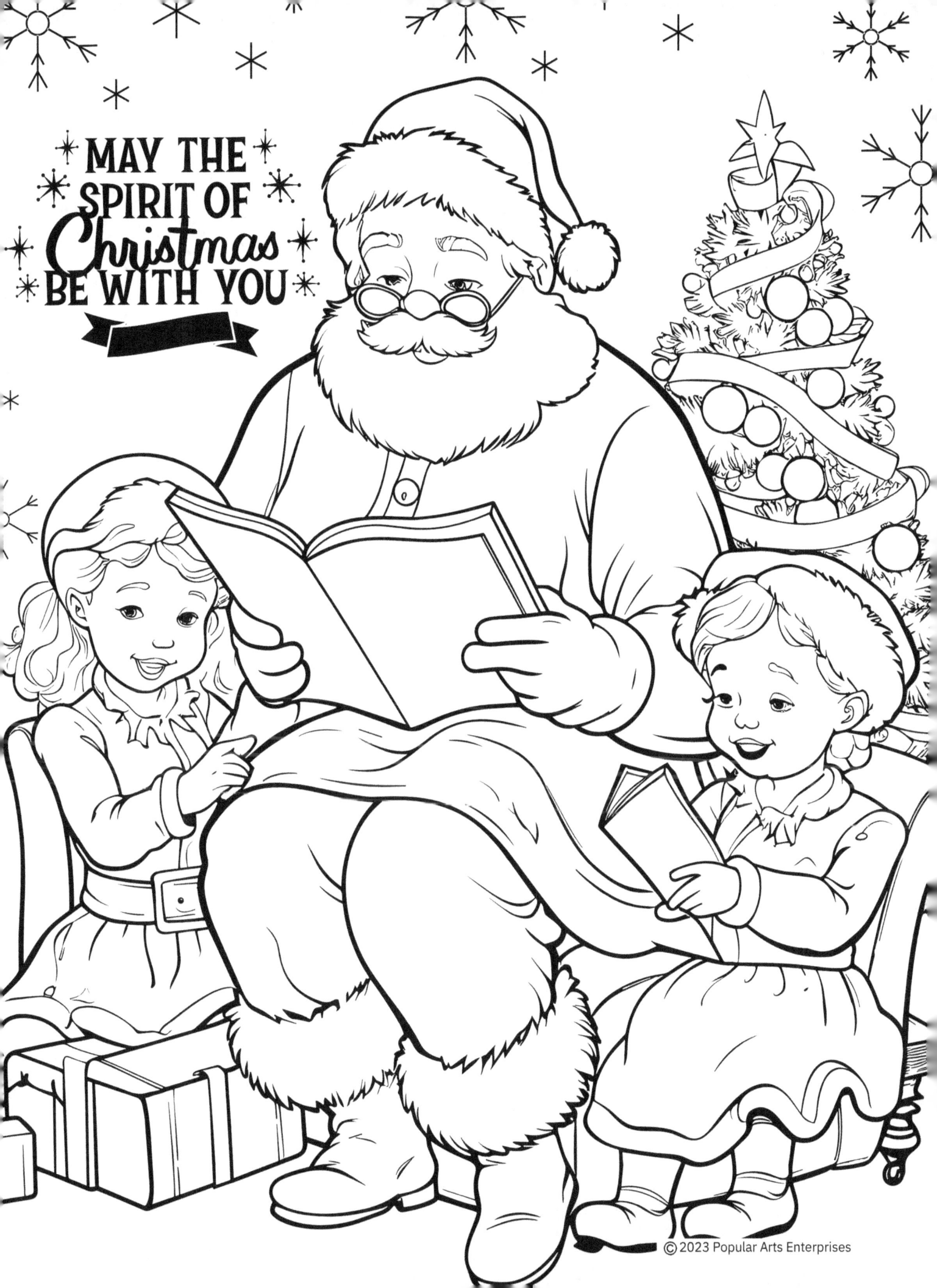

MAY THE SPIRIT OF *Christmas* BE WITH YOU

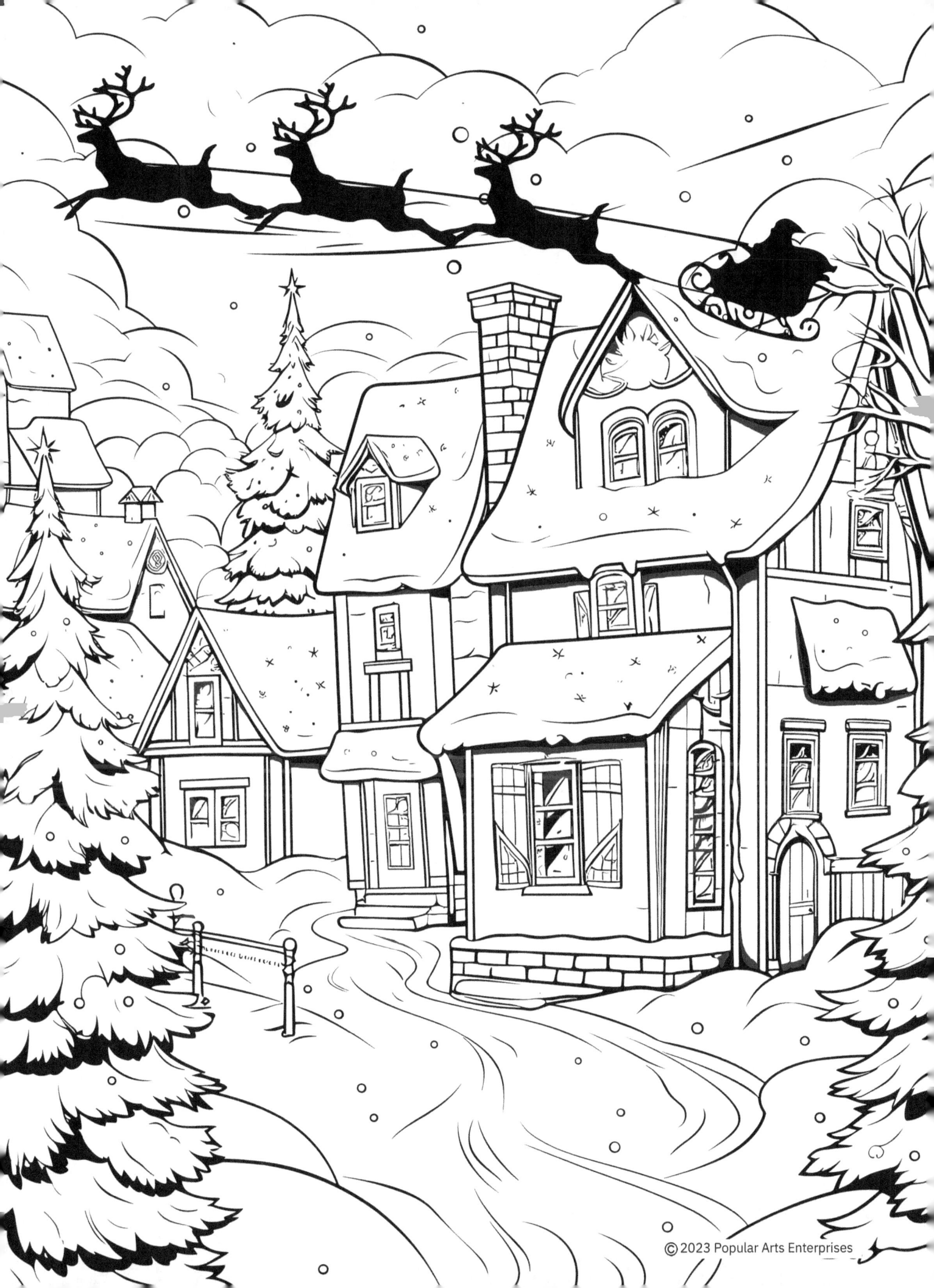

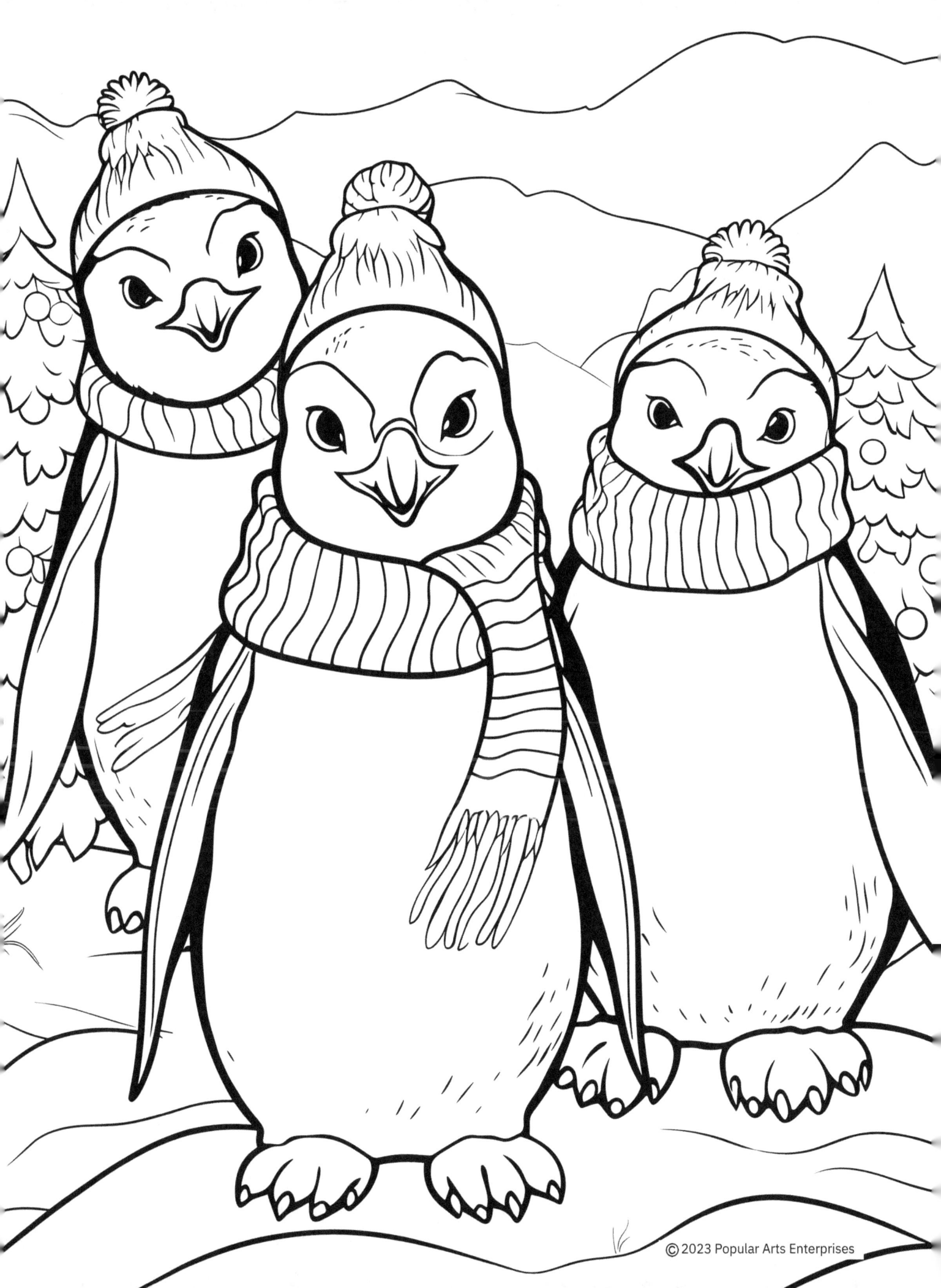

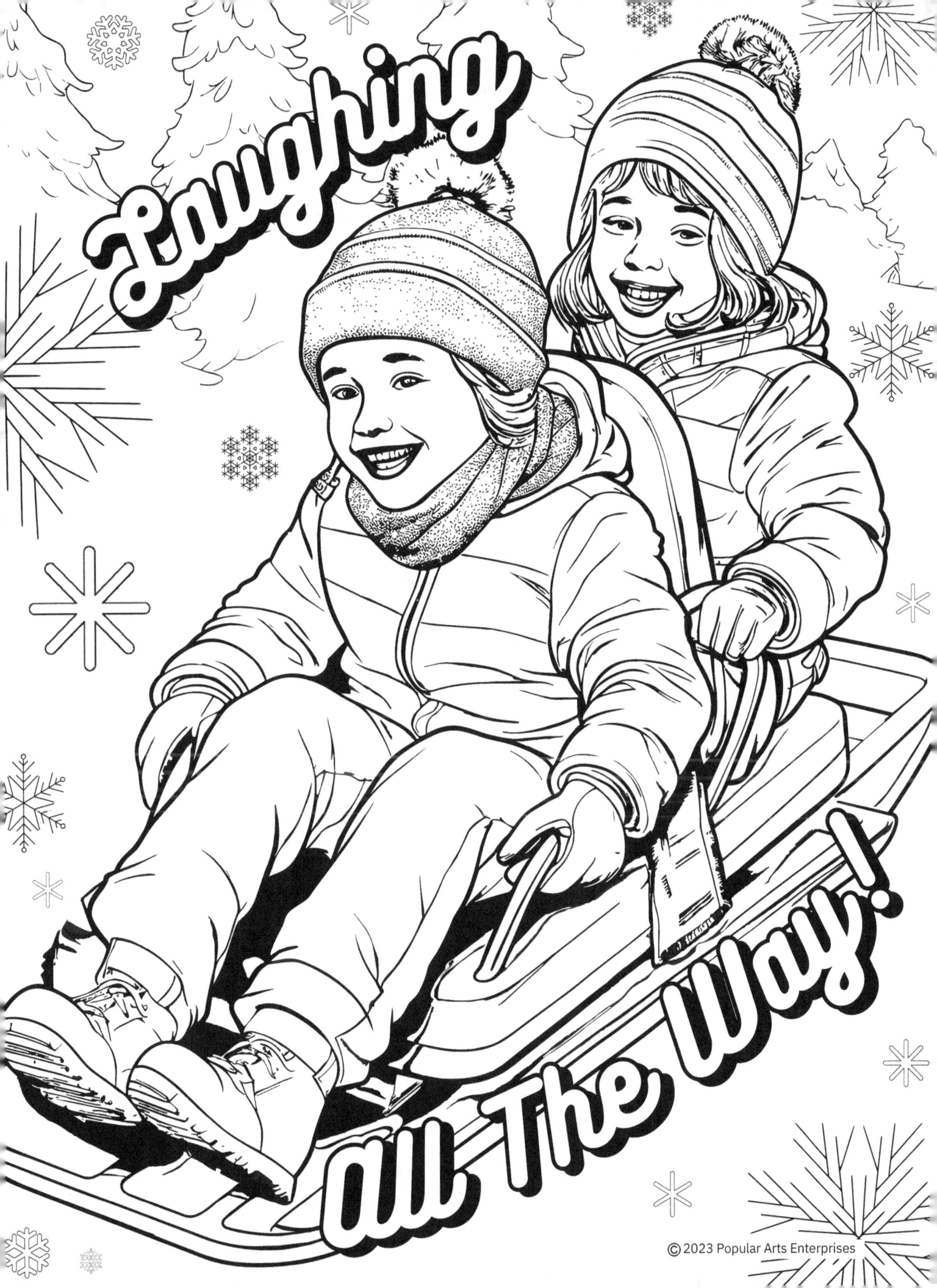

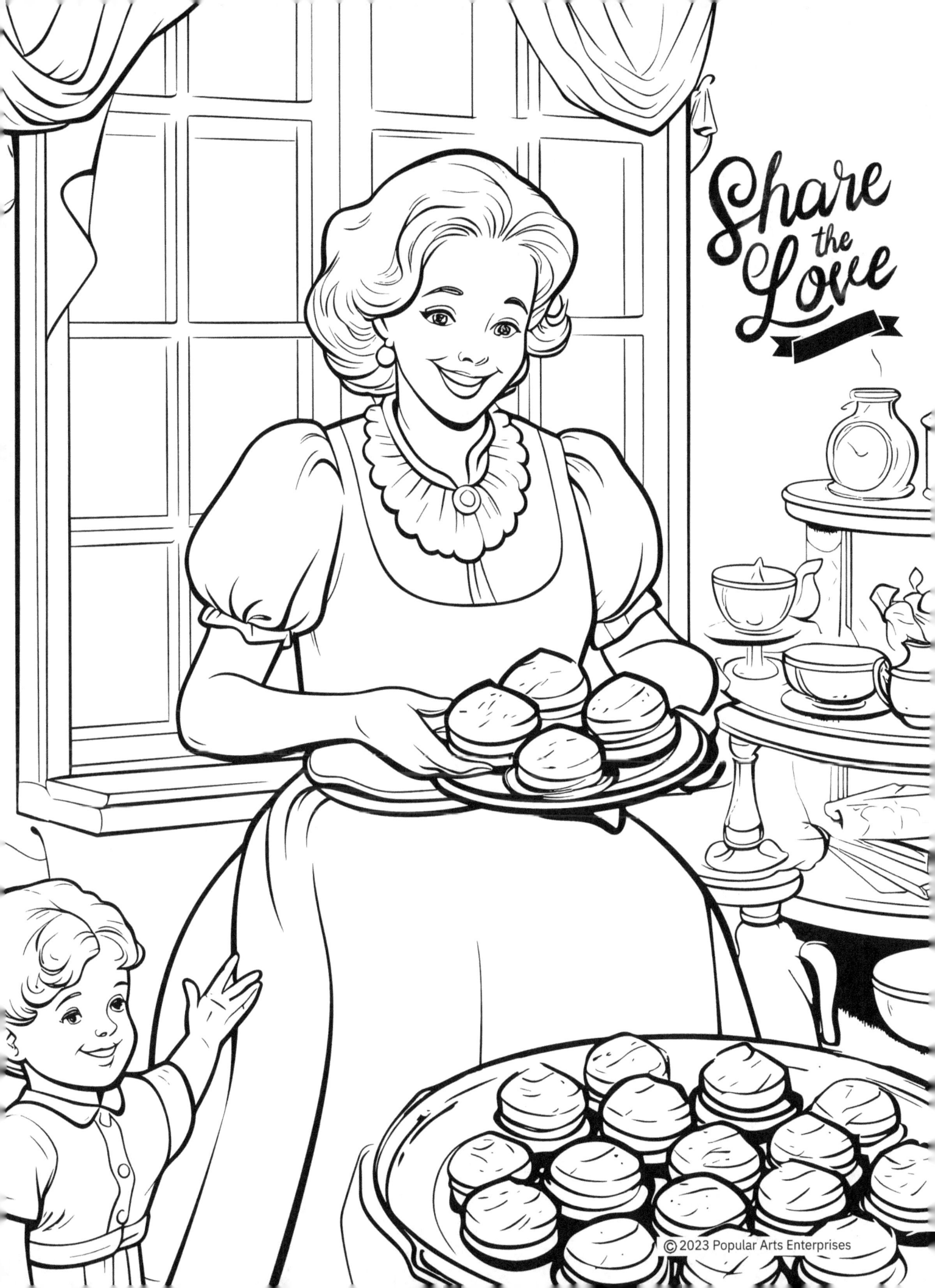

Share the Love

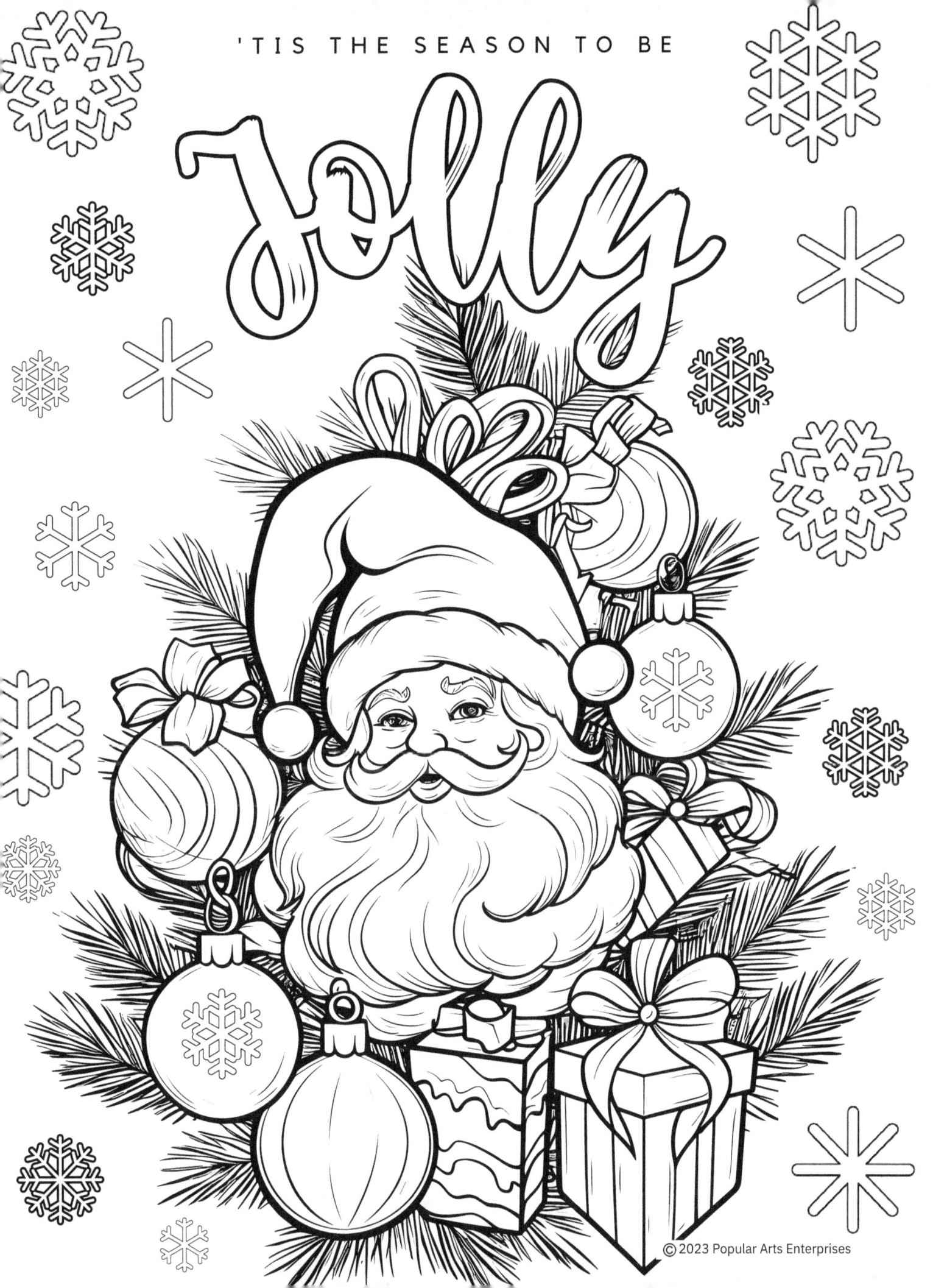

'TIS THE SEASON TO BE
Jolly

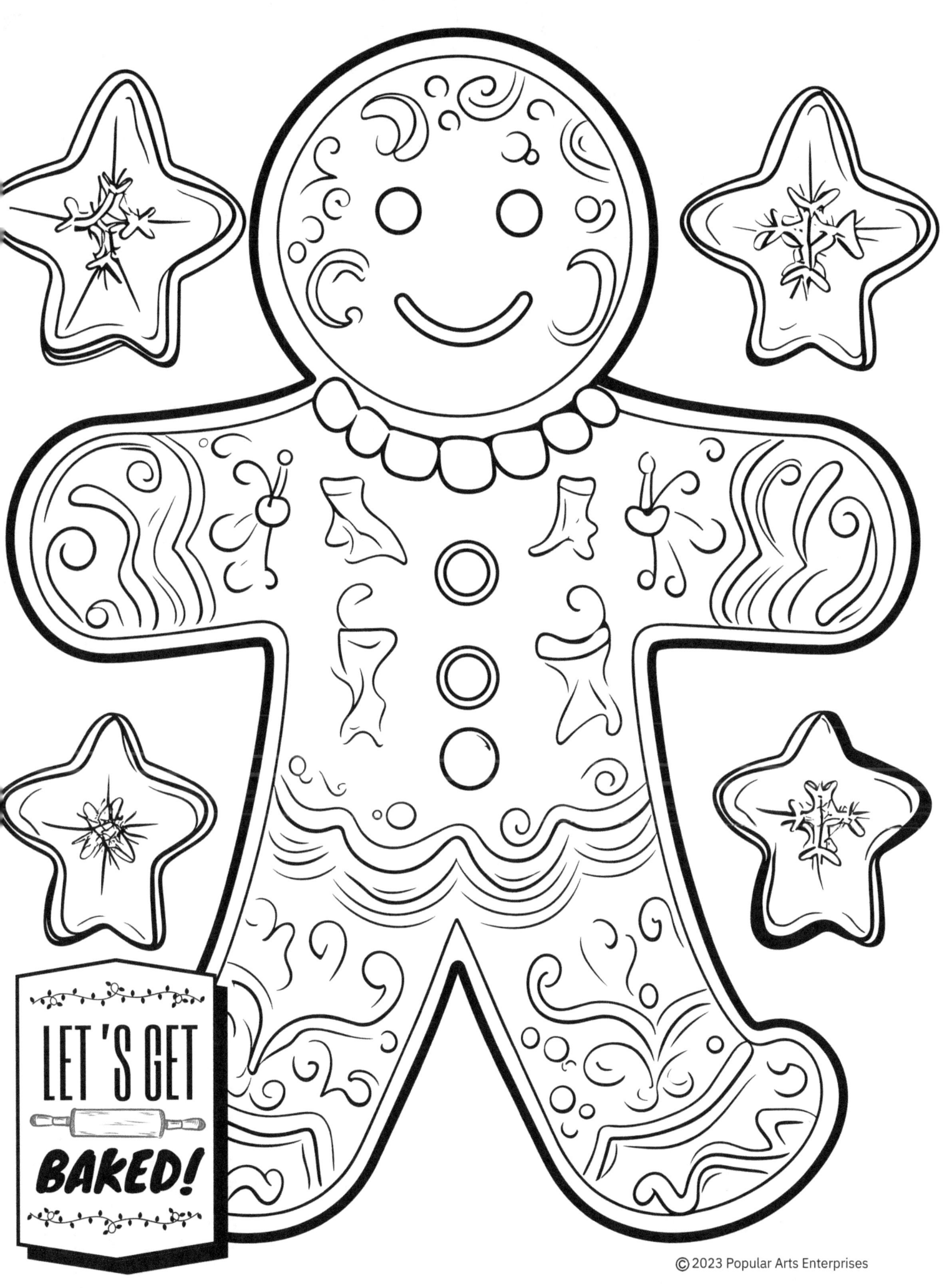

LET'S GET BAKED!

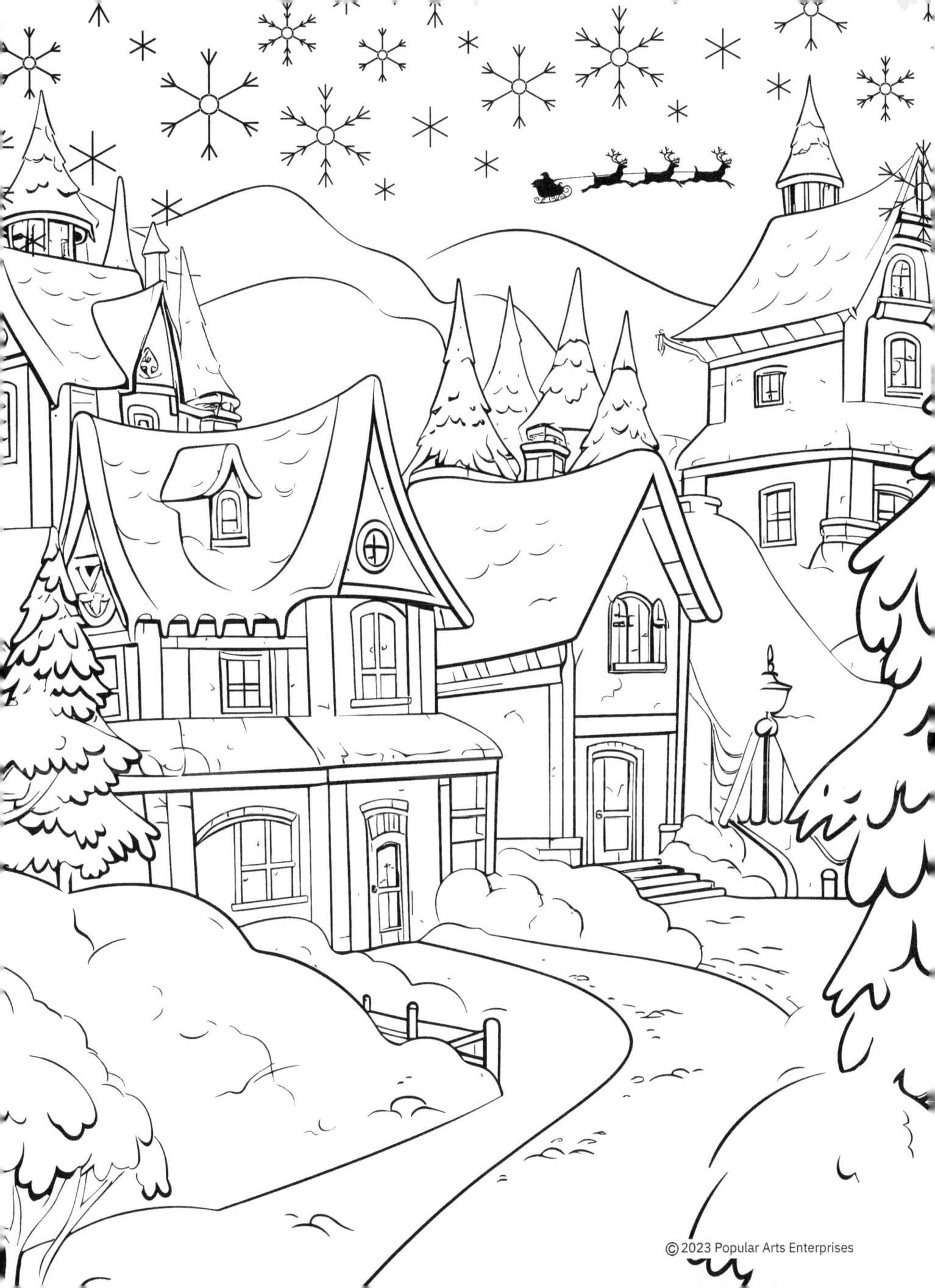

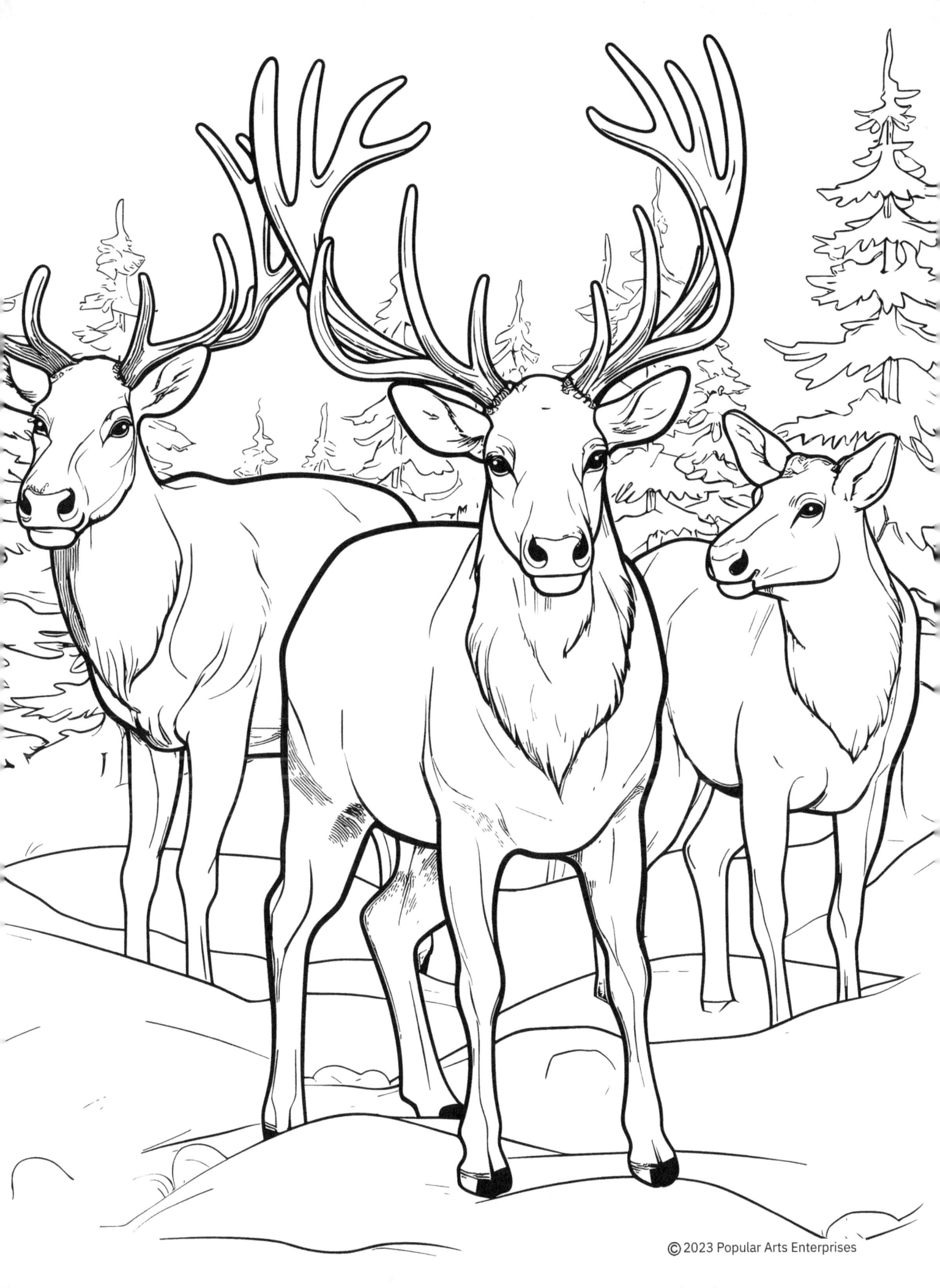

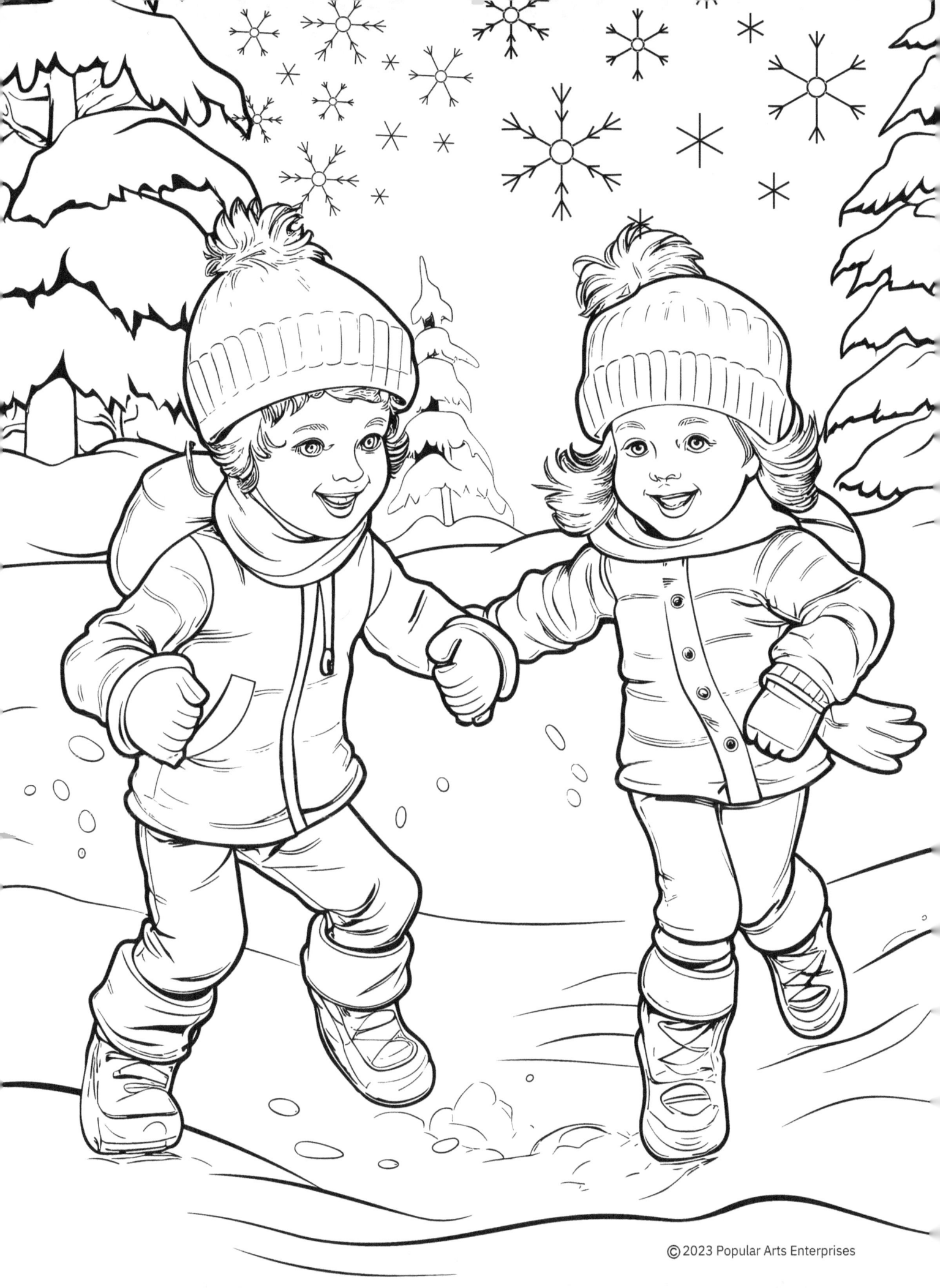

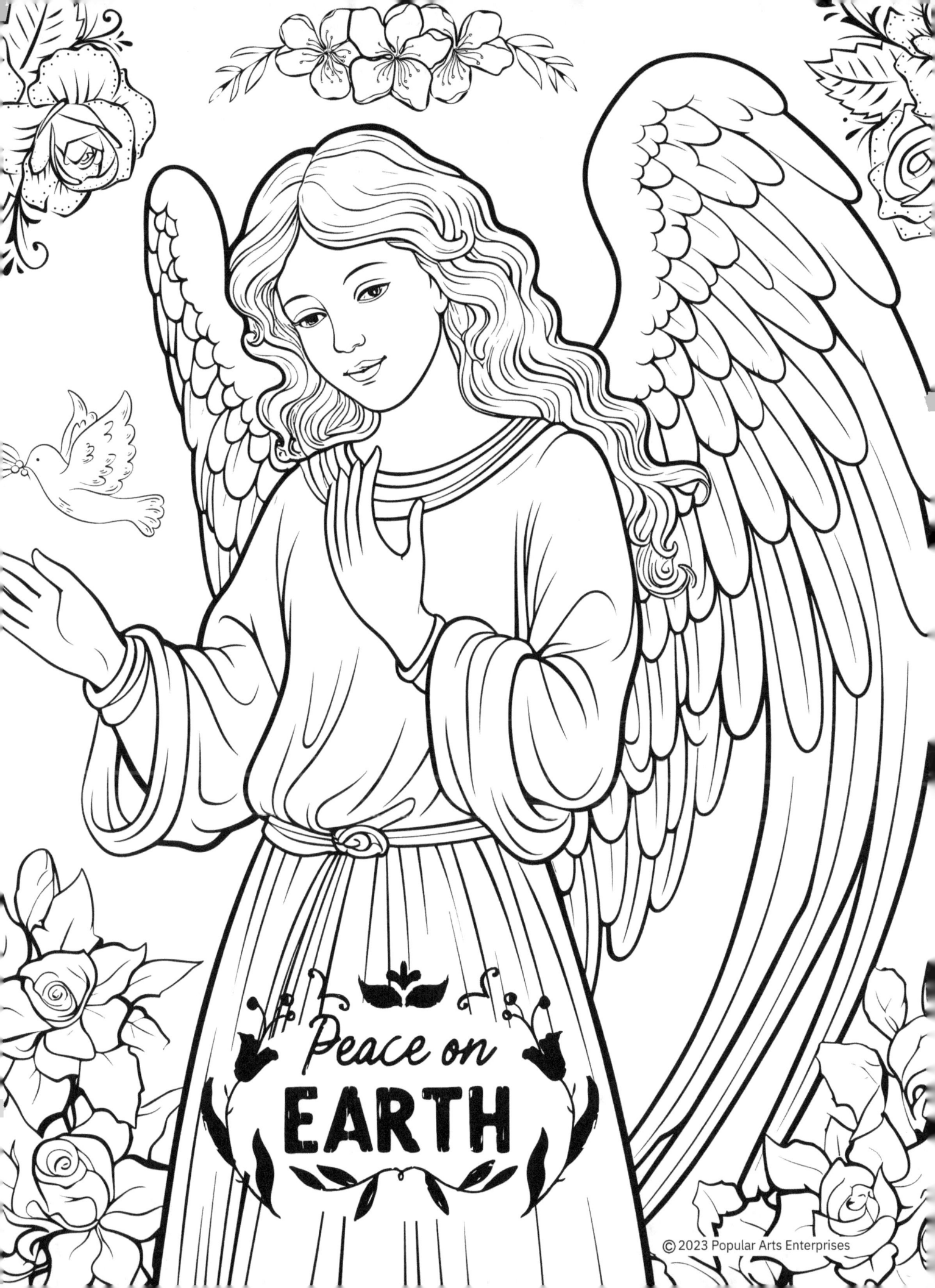

Peace on EARTH

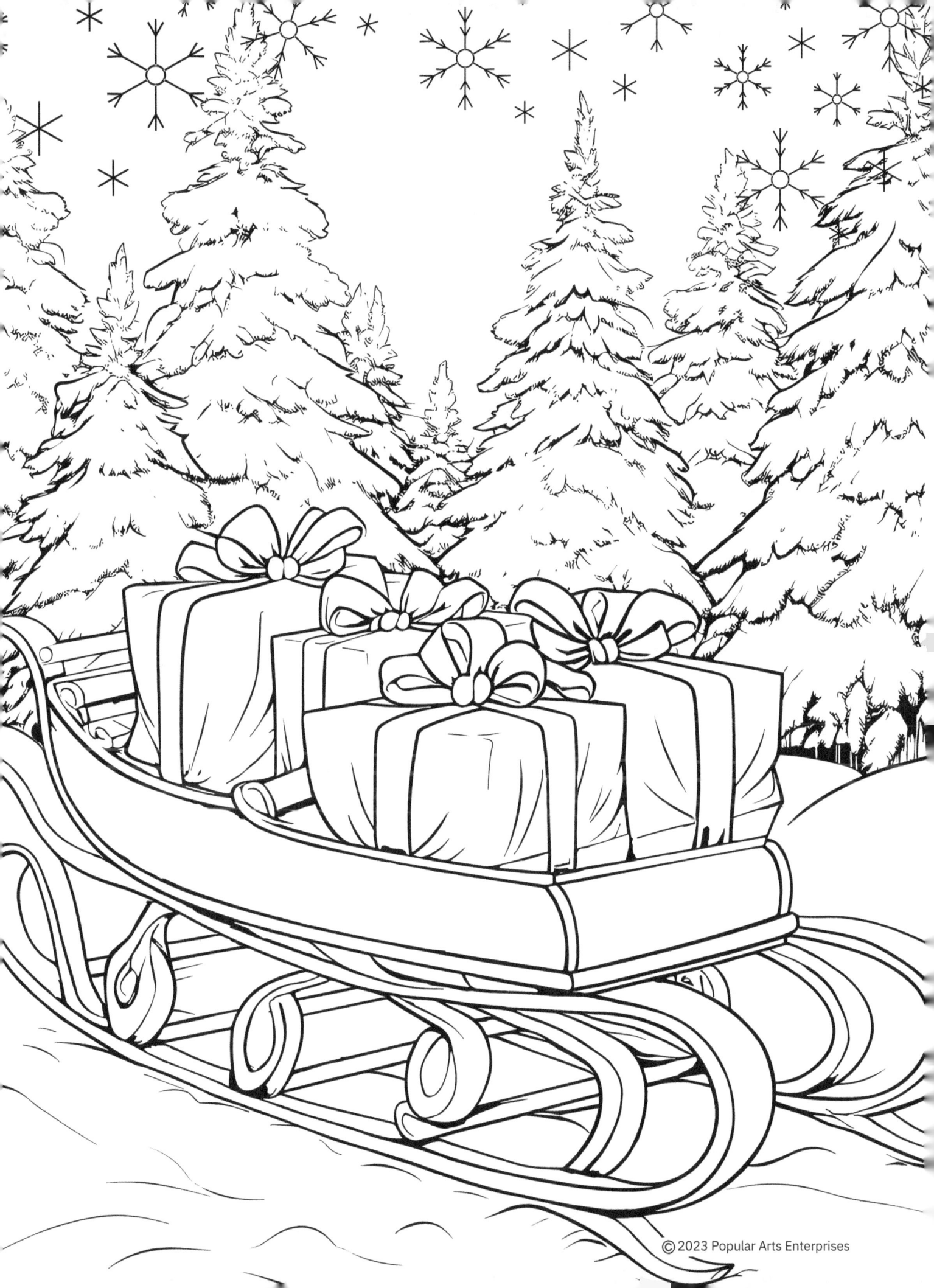

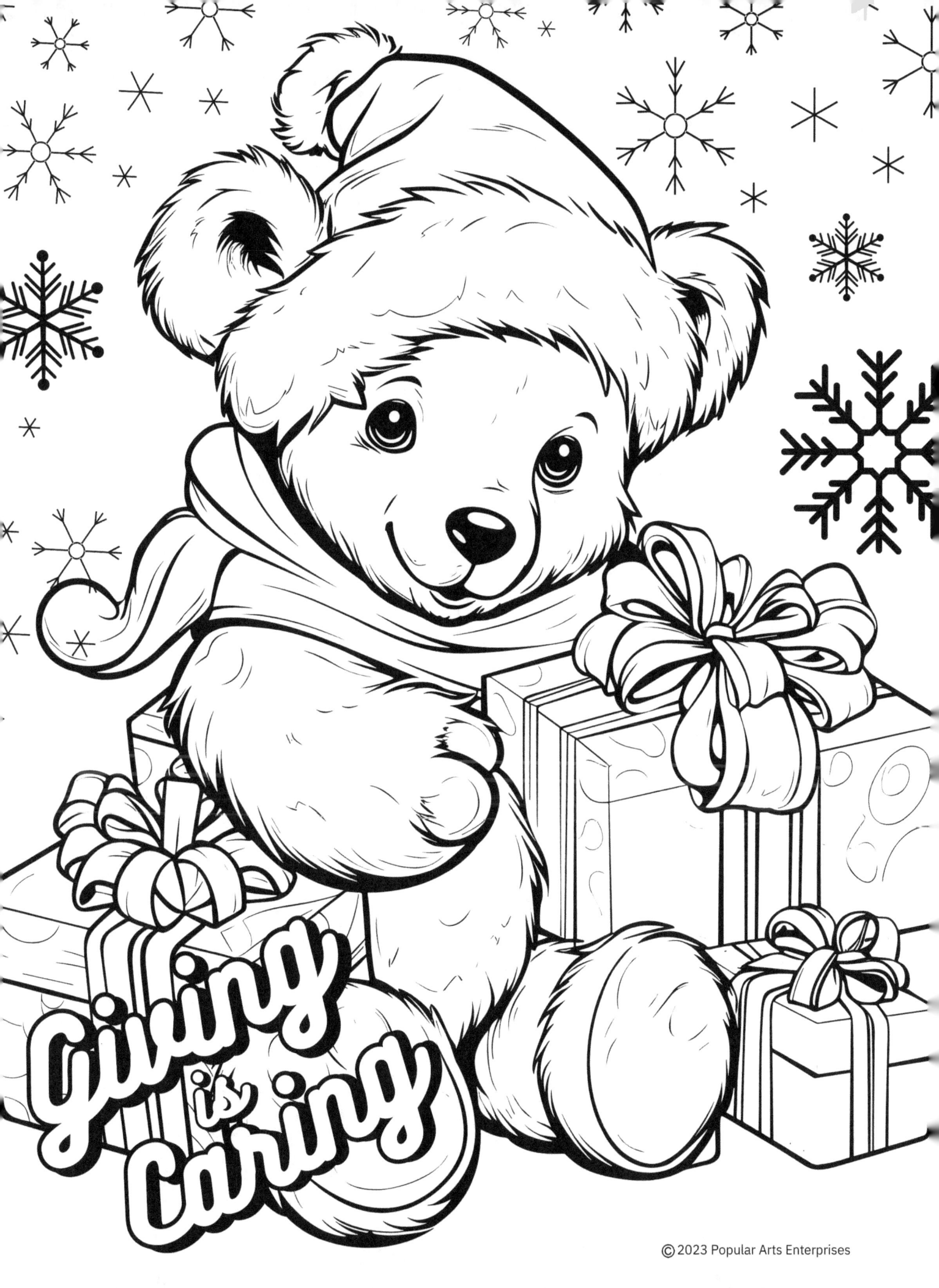

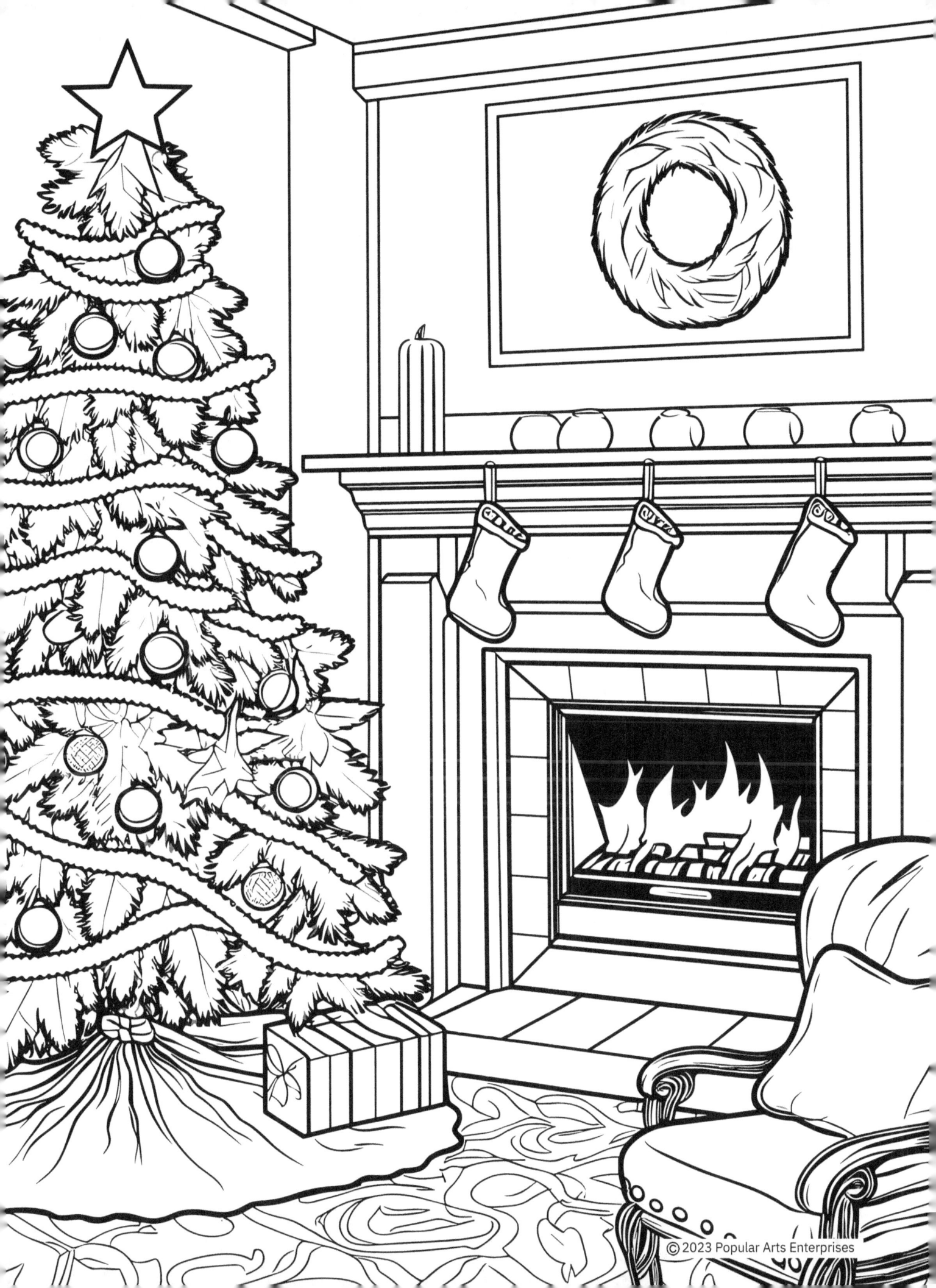

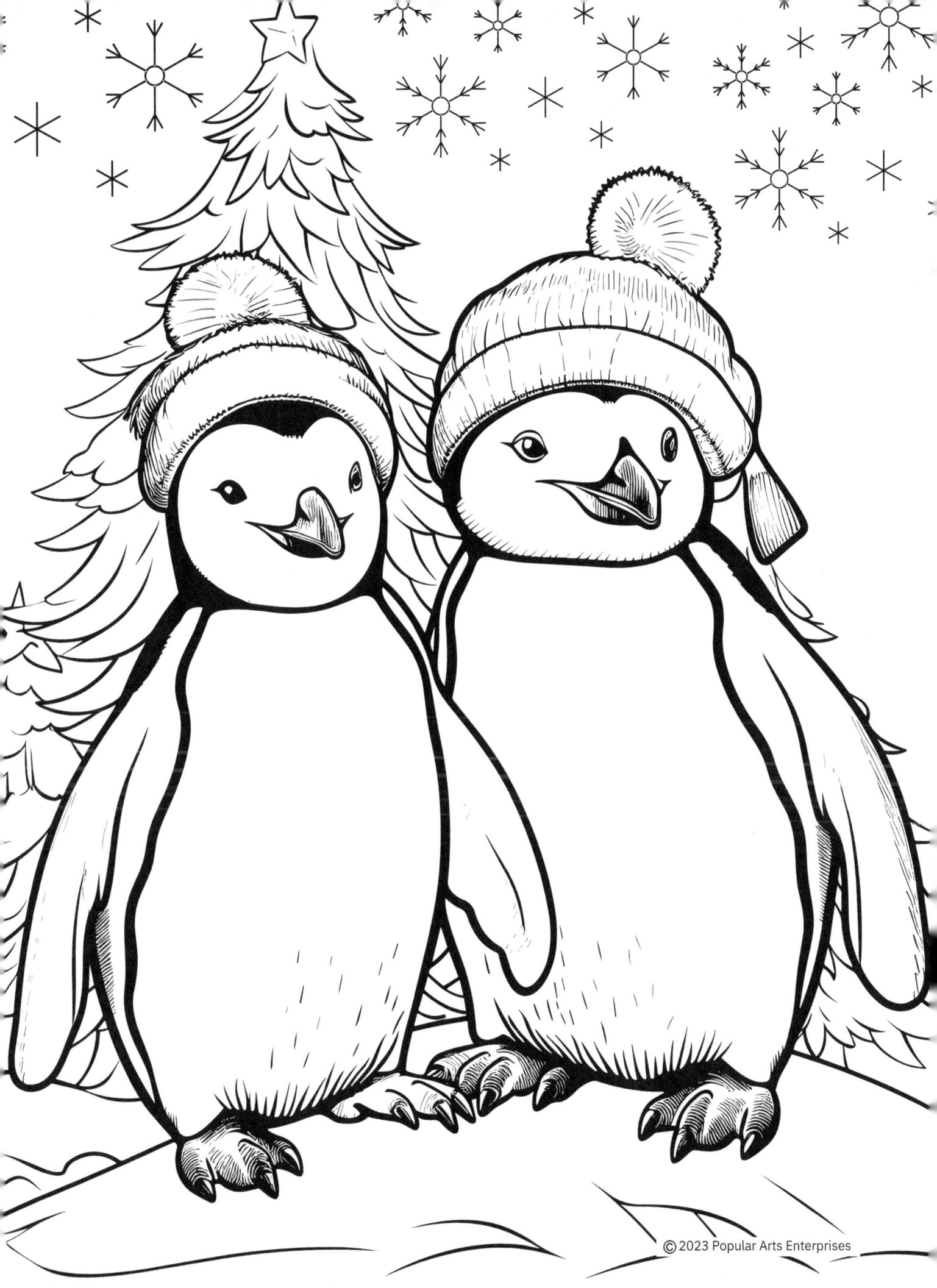

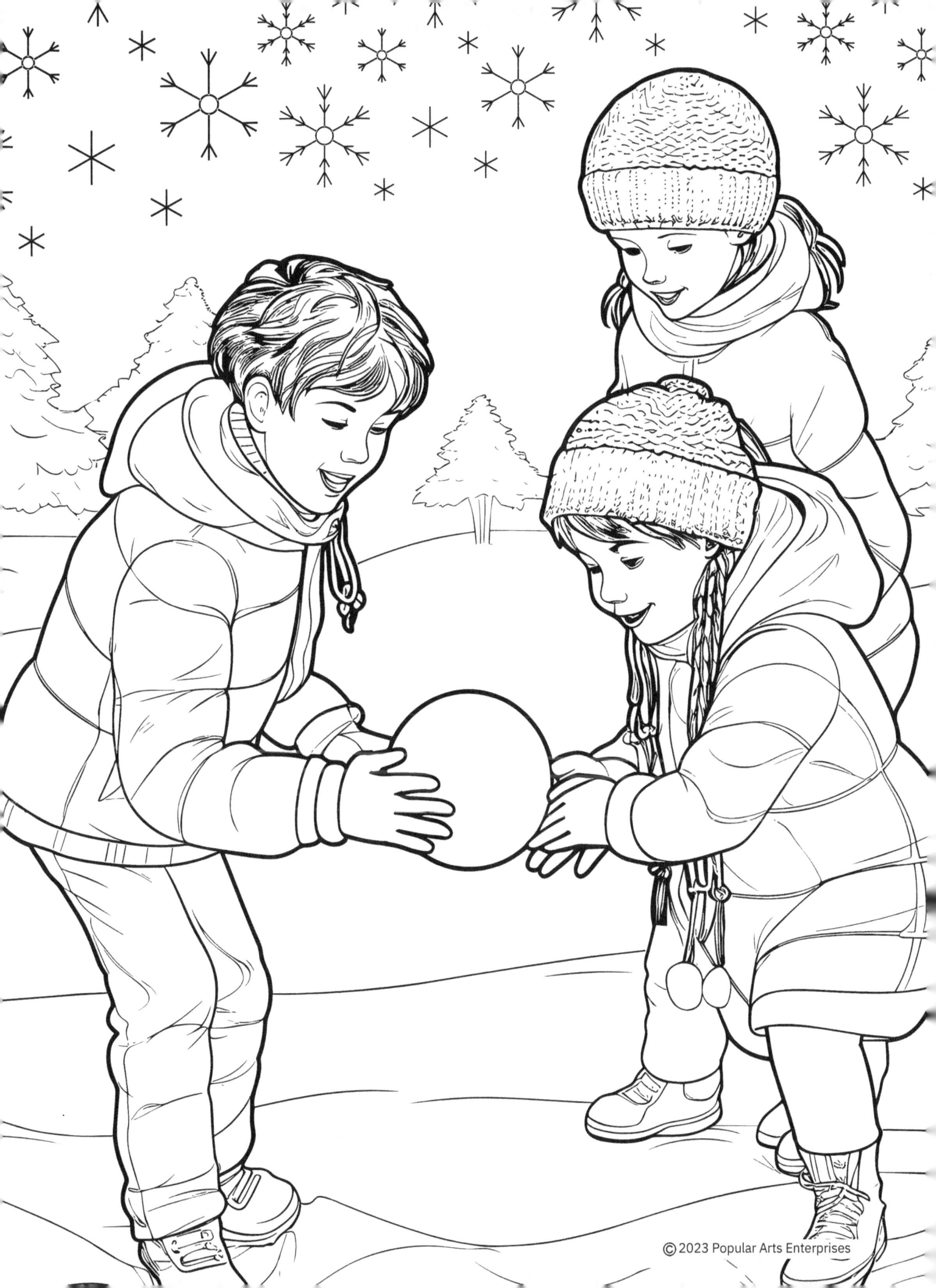

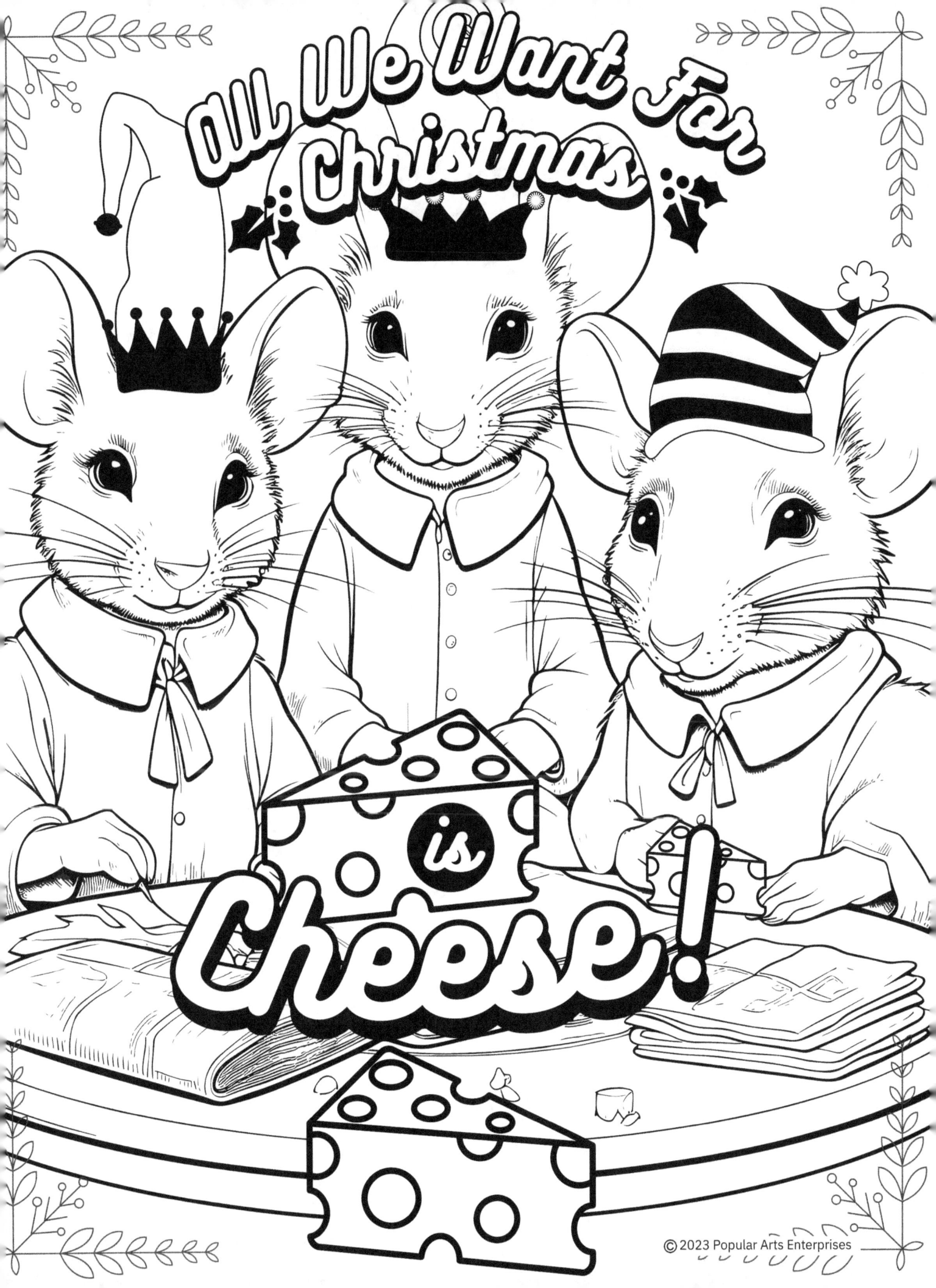

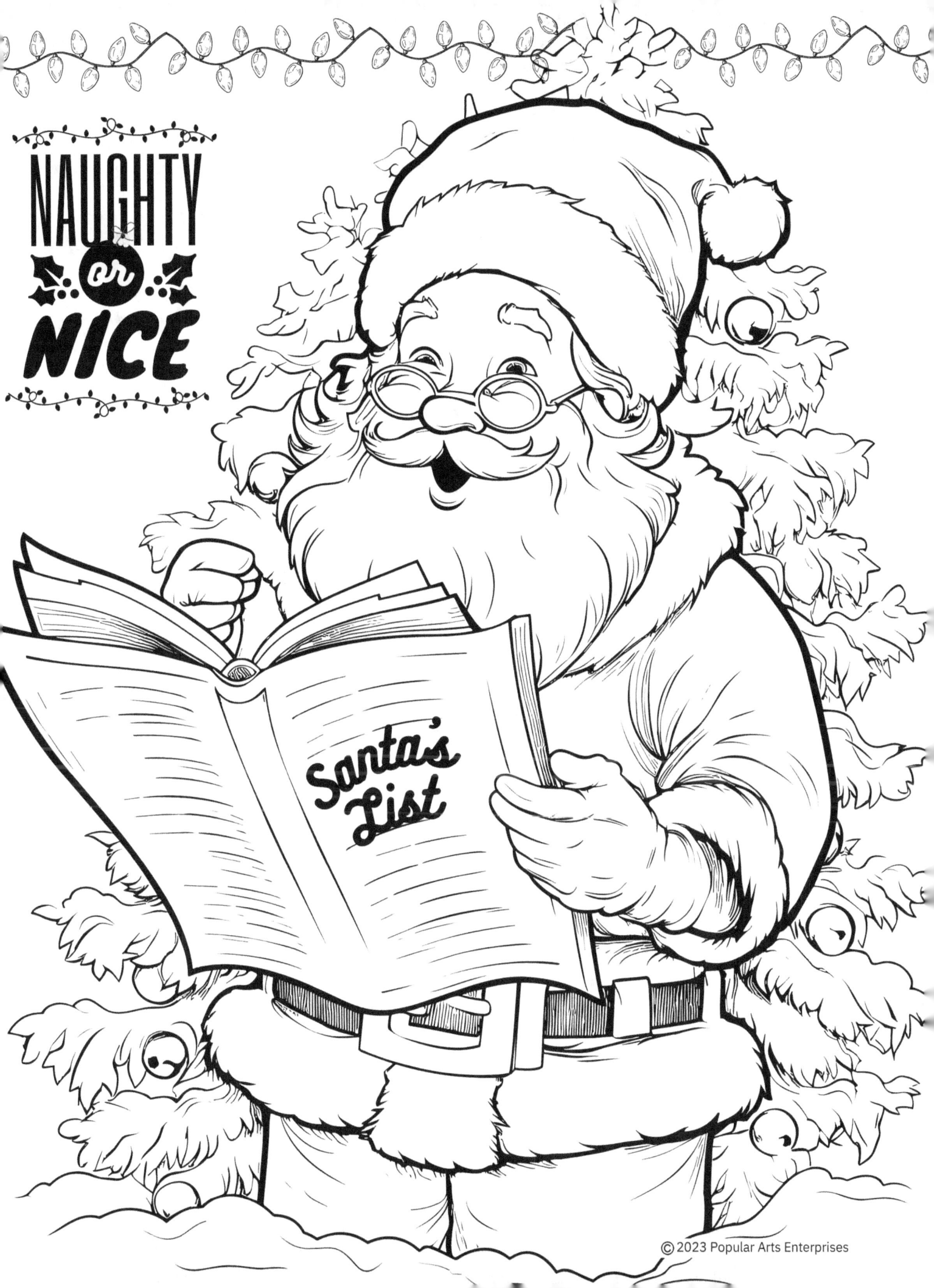

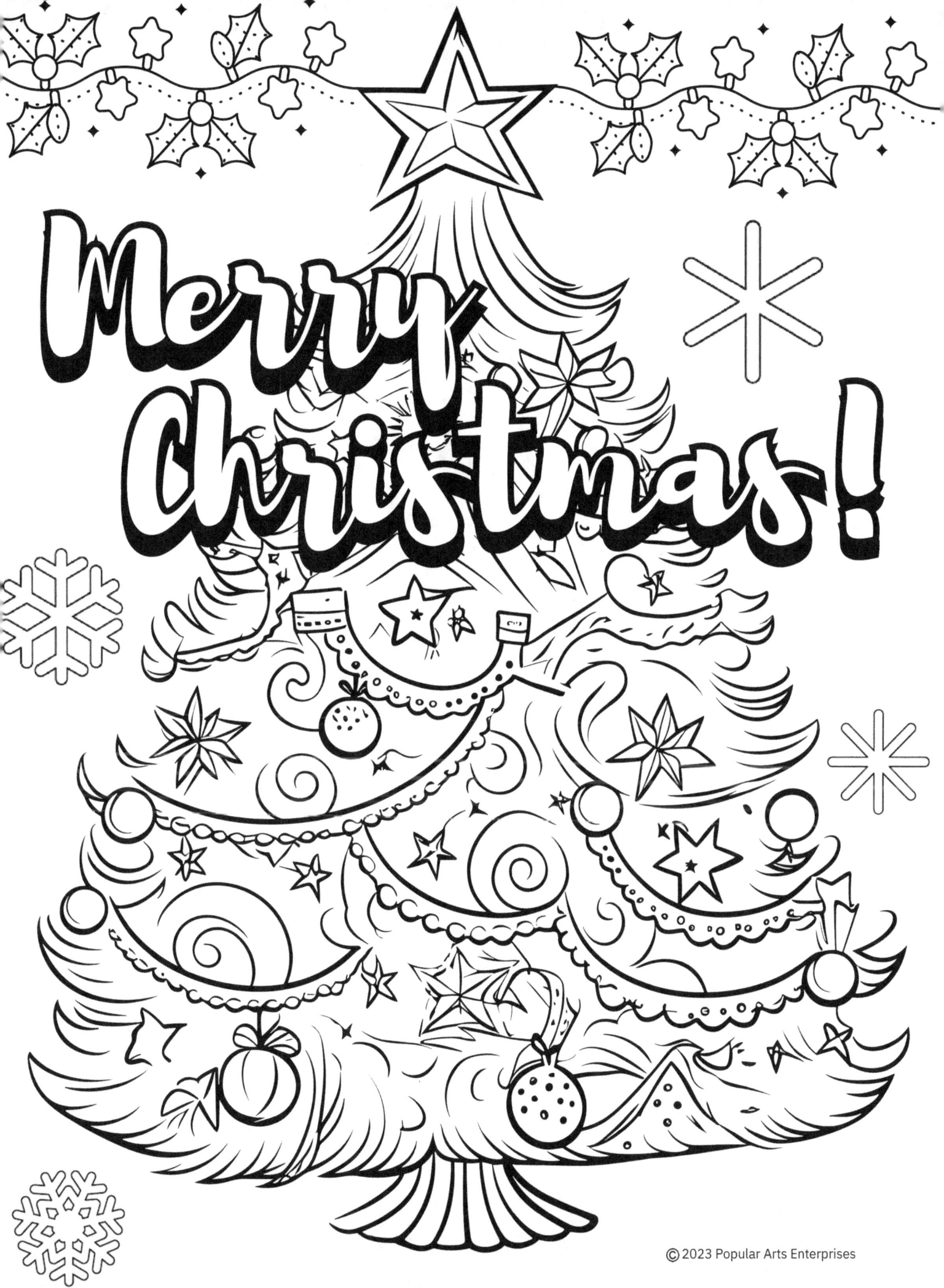

Thank You!

Don't be shy.... We want to hear from you!
We hope you enjoyed these fun and unique designs celebrating the spirit of Christmas.

Extra Bonus:
As our way of saying thanks we will email you, never before published, coloring pages. Takes 8 seconds!
(see below)

Here's how to receive your FREE 8 coloring book pages:

1 Please scan the QR code. Leave a review on Amazon and feel free to attach a picture of your masterpiece.

+

2 Tag your artwork and follow us on social media (see below).
*Must have at least 10+ followers.

=

TikTok: @popularartspublishing